A Year with Hekate:

Invocations,

Prayers, and Rituals for Every Day of the Year

Marcus Black

Chapter 1: Introduction
- Explanation of the purpose of the book
- Brief overview of Hekate and her role in history and mythology
- Explanation of the invocations, prayers, and rituals included in the book

Chapter 2: Prayers for January
- Prayer for each day of January, with a focus on new beginnings, fresh starts, and setting intentions for the new year
- Special new moon ritual for January, invoking Hekate as a guide and protector as we embark on our journey through the year

Chapter 3: Prayers for February
- Prayer for each day of February, with a focus on love, relationships, and connection
- Special full moon ritual for February, invoking Hekate as a guardian of love and compassion, and asking for her guidance in our relationships

Chapter 4: Prayers for March
- Prayer for each day of March, with a focus on growth, transformation, and renewal
- Special new moon ritual for March, invoking Hekate as a guide through the darkness of transformation and asking for her protection as we grow and change

Chapter 5: Prayers for April
- Prayer for each day of April, with a focus on abundance, prosperity, and fertility
- Special full moon ritual for April, invoking Hekate as a goddess of abundance and asking for her blessings on our finances, careers, and creative pursuits

Chapter 6: Prayers for May
- Prayer for each day of May, with a focus on beauty, creativity, and inspiration
- Special new moon ritual for May, invoking Hekate as a muse and asking for her inspiration and guidance in our creative endeavors

Chapter 7: Prayers for June
- Prayer for each day of June, with a focus on healing, health, and well-being
- Special full moon ritual for June, invoking Hekate as a healer and asking for her blessings on our physical, emotional, and spiritual health

Chapter 8: Prayers for July
- Prayer for each day of July, with a focus on protection, safety, and security

How to Use this Book

This book is more than a book. It is a year-long journey with the Dark Goddess. You will encounter her throughout the year. You will learn from her. You will grow with her as she takes you beyond what you thought you could be or who you thought you were. You can jump in at any time of the year.

When you turn the page and begin the journey, don't look back. Don't stop. Push through the day-to-day challenges of life, the humdrums of modernity, and focus for a just a little while each day on your relationship with the Goddess.

Be sure to start with the initiation ritual even if you already have a relationship with Hekate.

As you begin your time with her each day, find a quiet place. A space where the two of you can commune without being interrupted.

Gather a few candles (white and black) and some incense (myrrh).

Sit back quietly for a few minutes. Take a few deep slow breaths, then light the candles and the incense. When you are ready begin your prayer.

Then take a few moments to allow the presence of the Goddess saturate you. Listen for her to speak. Then make a note of your experience. Even if there are no apparent responses, make a note of it. Then watch through the day and week. Make notes of anything that you feel may be her way of communicating with you.

Chapter 1: Introduction

Welcome to "Hekate: Invocations, Prayers, and Rituals for Every Day of the Year". This devotional book is a daily guide for those seeking to connect with the goddess Hekate and incorporate her wisdom and guidance into their daily lives.

Hekate is a powerful and multifaceted goddess, known for her connections to magic, witchcraft, the underworld, and crossroads. She is also associated with wisdom, protection, and transformation. Throughout history and mythology, Hekate has been revered as a guide and mentor, offering her devotees the tools they need to navigate life's challenges with strength, courage, and grace.

This book is designed to help you deepen your connection with Hekate and cultivate a daily spiritual practice that incorporates her energy and influence. Each day, you will find an invocation or prayer to Hekate that can be used as a daily affirmation, mantra, or meditation. You will also find special new moon and full moon rituals that are designed to align with the cycles of the moon and harness Hekate's power.

By incorporating the daily practices and rituals in this book into your life, you can tap into Hekate's wisdom and guidance, and discover the strength and resilience that come from connecting with a powerful and wise goddess.

Brief overview of Hekate

Hekate is a complex and multifaceted goddess who has played a significant role in the history and mythology of many cultures throughout the centuries. Her origins can be traced back to ancient Greece, where she was often depicted as a three-headed goddess, with each head symbolizing a different aspect of her power and influence.

In Greek mythology, Hekate was associated with the underworld and the dead, as well as magic and witchcraft. She was believed to be able to cross between worlds, and was often called upon to help guide the souls of the dead to the afterlife. Hekate was also known as a goddess of the crossroads, symbolizing the many paths and choices that we face in life. She was said to be able to help people navigate difficult decisions and find the right path forward.

Throughout history, Hekate has been revered as a powerful and influential goddess, with many cultures and traditions incorporating her into their spiritual practices. In ancient Greece, she was often honored in household shrines and temples, and was also associated with fertility and childbirth. In the Roman Empire, Hekate was sometimes identified with the goddess Diana, and was often invoked as a protector of sailors and travelers.

In the Middle Ages and the Renaissance, Hekate became associated with witchcraft and the occult. She was often depicted in art and literature as a dark and mysterious figure, surrounded by symbols of magic and the supernatural. In many cultures, Hekate was seen as a goddess of transformation, helping people to overcome obstacles and find their true path in life.

Today, Hekate is often seen as a guide and mentor, offering wisdom, protection, and transformation to those who seek her out. She is revered by many modern pagan and witchcraft traditions, and is often called upon in rituals and ceremonies.

Many people also see Hekate as a symbol of female empowerment, and look to her as a source of strength and resilience in their own lives.

Whether you are new to Hekate or have been a devotee for years, this book offers a daily practice that can deepen your connection with this powerful goddess and help you tap into her wisdom and guidance. By incorporating the daily practices and rituals in this book into your life, you can discover the strength and resilience that come from connecting with a powerful and wise goddess.

Explanation of the prayers, and rituals included in the book

The prayers, and rituals included in this book are designed to help you deepen your connection with Hekate and incorporate her energy and influence into your daily life. Each day, you will find an invocation or prayer to Hekate that can be used as a daily affirmation, mantra, or meditation. These invocations and prayers are intended to help you focus your energy and intentions, and connect with Hekate's wisdom and guidance.

In addition to the daily prayers, the book also includes special new moon rituals that are designed to align with the cycles of the moon and harness Hekate's power. The new moon ritual is focused on setting intentions and manifesting your desires, while the full moon ritual is focused on releasing negative energy and emotions, and inviting in positivity and abundance.

Each ritual includes detailed instructions for setting up your altar, casting a circle, and invoking Hekate's energy. The rituals also include suggestions for specific herbs, crystals, and other tools that can be used to enhance the power of the ritual. The book also includes guidance on how to close the circle and properly dispose of any materials used in the ritual.

The invocations, prayers, and rituals in this book are designed to be accessible to people of all spiritual backgrounds and experience levels. Whether you are new to Hekate or have been a devotee for years, these practices can help you deepen your connection with this powerful goddess and tap into her wisdom and guidance. By incorporating these practices into your daily life, you can cultivate a sense of inner strength, resilience, and empowerment, and navigate life's challenges with grace and confidence.

Let's begin by introducing ourselves to Hekate

An initiation ritual is a powerful way to formally introduce yourself to Hekate and begin your journey with her. Here is ritual that you can use to connect with the goddess:

Materials:

- A black candle
- A bowl of water
- An offering of your choice (such as herbs, crystals, or food)
- Incense (such as frankincense or myrrh)
- A picture or statue of Hekate (optional)

Preparation:

- Choose a quiet, private space where you will not be disturbed.

- Set up your altar with the black candle, bowl of water, offering, and incense.

- Light the incense and the black candle.

Ritual:

1. Begin by taking a few deep breaths and centering yourself. Close your eyes and visualize yourself standing at a crossroads, with Hekate standing before you.

2. Light the black candle and say, "Hekate, I invite you to join me in this space. I seek to connect with your wisdom and guidance."

3. Hold your hands over the bowl of water and say, "I offer this water as a symbol of my willingness to open myself up to your influence and guidance."

4. Place your offering on the altar and say, "I offer this [name of offering] as a symbol of my gratitude and respect for you, Hekate."

5. Take a few moments to gaze at the picture or statue of Hekate (if you have one). If you do not have one, you can simply visualize her in your mind's eye. Say, "Hekate, I am here to connect with you and learn from you. I am open to your guidance and willing to do the work to deepen our relationship."

6. Spend a few minutes in meditation or prayer, focusing on your intention to connect with Hekate and inviting her energy into your life.

7. When you feel ready, thank Hekate for her presence and blow out the black candle. Leave the other elements on the altar as an offering to Hekate.

After the ritual, take some time to reflect on your experience and any insights or feelings that came up. You can repeat this ritual as often as you like, whenever you feel the need to deepen your connection with Hekate.

Notes on Your Initial Contact with Hekate

Chapter 2: Prayers for January

In this chapter, you will find a collection of invocations and prayers to Hekate that are specifically tailored to the energy and themes of this month.

These daily affirmations and meditations are designed to help you connect with Hekate's energy and tap into her wisdom and guidance as you navigate the challenges and opportunities of the new year.

Remember to light a candle, offer some myrrh incense and a bowl of water each day.

Day 1: Hekate, guide me as I begin anew. Help me to release what no longer serves me and step into a new phase of growth and expansion.

Day 2: Hekate, grant me the strength to overcome any obstacles that come my way. Help me to stay grounded and centered as I navigate this journey.

Day 3: Hekate, grant me clarity and focus as I set my intentions for the year ahead. Help me to stay aligned with my purpose and take bold steps towards my dreams.

Day 4: Hekate, guide me as I shed old skin and step into a new version of myself. Help me to embrace change and transformation with courage and grace.

Day 5: Hekate, grant me the gift of intuition and insight as I navigate this journey. Help me to listen deeply to my inner voice and trust the guidance that arises.

Day 6: Hekate, surround me with your protective energy as I move forward on my path. Help me to feel safe and secure as I navigate the challenges of the year ahead.

Day 7: Hekate, inspire me with your creative energy and help me to manifest my vision in the world. Guide me as I express my authentic self and share my gifts with others.

Day 8: Hekate, bless me with your energy of abundance and prosperity. Help me to recognize and receive the blessings that are already present in my life, and to manifest even more abundance in the year ahead.

Day 9: Hekate, guide me as I shed old habits and patterns and step into a new level of growth and expansion. Help me to recognize and release any limitations that are holding me back, and to step fully into my power.

Day 10: Hekate, bless me with your energy of healing and renewal. Help me to prioritize my wellbeing and cultivate practices that restore and rejuvenate me. Guide me as I tend to my physical, emotional, and spiritual health.

Day 11: Hekate, bless my intentions and actions as I manifest my dreams in the world. Help me to stay aligned with my highest vision and to take inspired action towards my goals.

Day 12: Hekate, guide me as I move forward into the unknown. Help me to trust the journey and to stay connected to my inner wisdom and guidance. Protect me from any harm or negativity that may arise.

Day 13: Hekate, grant me clarity and discernment as I make decisions and take action in my life. Help me to see clearly and to choose the path that is in alignment with my highest good and purpose.

Day 14: Hekate, guide me as I release old patterns and embrace new levels of growth and transformation. Help me to let go of what no longer serves me and to step fully into my power and purpose.

Day 15: Hekate, bless me with your energy of manifestation and abundance. Help me to align with the energy of prosperity and to attract wealth and abundance in all areas of my life.

Day 16: Hekate, surround me with your protective energy and keep me safe from harm. Help me to feel grounded and secure as I navigate the challenges of the year ahead.

Day 17: Hekate, inspire me with your creative energy and help me to express my unique gifts and talents in the world. Guide me as I share my creativity with others and make a positive impact.

Day 18: Hekate, guide me as I shed old skin and embrace new beginnings in my journey. Bless me with your energy of transformation and renewal as I release what no longer serves me and step into a new phase of growth and evolution.

Day 19: Hekate, bless me with your energy of courage and strength as I navigate the challenges of this year. Help me to tap into my inner resilience and to overcome any obstacle that comes my way.

Day 20: Hekate, guide me as I step into new territory in my life. Protect me from any harm or negativity that may arise, and help me to trust the journey and stay connected to my inner wisdom and intuition.

Day 21: Hekate, bless me with your energy of manifestation and abundance. Help me to align with the energy of prosperity and to manifest my desires into reality in all areas of my life.

Day 22: Hekate, guide me as I shed old patterns and embrace new levels of growth and evolution in my life. Help me to step into my power and purpose with clarity and confidence.

Day 23: Hekate, surround me with your protective energy and keep me safe from harm. Help me to feel grounded and secure as I navigate the challenges of the year ahead.

Day 24: Hekate, inspire me with your creative energy and help me to express my unique gifts and talents in the world. Guide me as I share my creativity with others and make a positive impact.

Day 25: Prayer: Hekate, bless me with your energy of manifestation and abundance. Help me to attract wealth and prosperity in all areas of my life.

Day 26: Hekate, guide me as I release old patterns and embrace new levels of growth and transformation. Help me to let go of what no longer serves me and to step fully into my power and purpose.

Day 27: Hekate, surround me with your protective energy and guide me as I navigate the unknown territory of this new year. Help me to trust the journey and to stay connected to my inner wisdom and intuition.

Day 28: Hekate, bless me with your energy of healing and transformation. Help me to release any emotional or spiritual blocks that may be holding me back and to step into a space of wholeness and healing.

Day 29: Hekate, bless me with your energy of manifestation and abundance. Help me to attract new opportunities and blessings in all areas of my life and to align with the energy of prosperity.

Day 30: Hekate, surround me with your protective energy and keep me safe from harm. Help me to stay strong and resilient in the face of any challenges or obstacles that may arise.

Day 31: Hekate, guide me as I reflect on the past year and set intentions for the new year. Bless me with your energy of transformation and renewal as I release what no longer serves me and step into a new phase of growth and evolution.

New moon ritual for January

Find a quiet, dark space where you can connect with the energy of the new moon. Light a candle, incense, and a bowl of water. Take a few deep breaths to center yourself.

Invocation to Hekate

Hekate, great goddess of the crossroads, Mistress of magic and the unseen, I call upon your presence here tonight To guide and protect me on my journey.

You who hold the keys to the mysteries, You who guide souls through the underworld, I ask for your guidance and your wisdom As I navigate the twists and turns of life.

Hekate, guardian of the night, I ask that you surround me with your protective energy And keep me safe from harm and negativity.

Bless me with your magic and your power, Help me to tap into the depths of my own inner wisdom, And to trust my intuition as I move forward.

Hekate, I call upon you now To be my guide, my protector, and my friend As I journey through this new year.

Close your eyes and visualize a path stretching out before you. You stand at the beginning of this path, ready to embark on a new journey through the year.

As you begin to walk, feel the energy of Hekate surrounding you. Visualize her standing at the crossroads ahead, waiting to guide you on your journey.

Approach her with an offering of your choice, perhaps a small piece of bread, a flower, or a piece of jewelry. Speak your intentions for the year aloud, asking for her guidance and protection as you move forward.

When you feel ready, ask Hekate to bless you with her energy of transformation, renewal, manifestation, and protection. Take a few deep breaths and allow yourself to feel her energy flowing through you.

When you are ready, thank Hekate for her presence and guidance, and release any fears or doubts that may be holding you back. Allow yourself to feel empowered and ready to take on whatever challenges or opportunities come your way.

Extinguish the candle and spend some time reflecting on your experience. Know that Hekate is always with you, guiding and protecting you on your journey through the year.

Chapter 3: Invocations and Prayers for February

As the second month of the year, February brings a sense of renewal and hope for the coming months. In this chapter, we will explore invocations and prayers for February that focus on love, compassion, and inner strength. Let us call upon the energy of Hekate to guide us through this month and help us tap into our own inner power.

Day 1: Hekate, hear our prayer on this day, As we seek your guidance and blessings. May we be filled with love and compassion, And may our relationships be filled with joy and fulfillment.

Day 2: Hekate, we offer our prayers to you, On this day of transformation and change. May our relationships be strengthened, And may we be filled with love and compassion.

Day 3: Hekate, hear our prayer on this day, As we seek your guidance and wisdom. May we be filled with love and compassion, And may our relationships be blessed with joy and harmony.

Day 4: Hekate, we offer our prayers to you, On this day of choice and decision. May our relationships be filled with love and compassion, And may we find joy and fulfillment in our connections.

Day 5: Hekate, hear our prayer on this day, As we seek your protection and guidance. May our relationships be blessed with love and harmony, And may we be filled with joy and fulfillment.

Day 6: Hekate, we offer our prayers to you, On this day of release and healing. May our relationships be filled with love and compassion, And may we find joy and fulfillment in our connections.

Day 7: Hekate, hear our prayer on this day, As we seek your guidance and blessings. May our relationships be filled with love and compassion, And may we find joy and fulfillment in our connections.

Day 8: Hekate, goddess of the night and the moon, We call upon you on this day, To help us tap into the wisdom of the cycles of nature. Guide us in creating loving and healthy relationships, And help us to find joy and fulfillment in our connections.

Day 9: Hekate, we offer this prayer to you on this day of love. As the goddess of the moon and the night, you hold the power of transformation and renewal. We ask that you help us release any old patterns or negative energies that may be blocking our ability to connect with others in a healthy and loving way.

Day 10: Help us to recognize the beauty and value in ourselves and in those around us, and to foster relationships that are based on mutual respect and love. May our hearts be open to give and receive, and may the bonds we form be strong and enduring.

Day 11: Hekate, may we communicate with compassion and empathy, and may we always seek to lift each other up. May your divine love inspire us to be the best versions of ourselves, and to support one another in all of our endeavors.

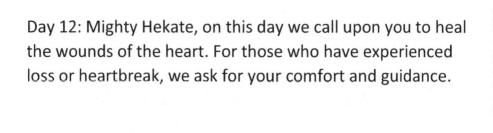

Day 12: Mighty Hekate, on this day we call upon you to heal the wounds of the heart. For those who have experienced loss or heartbreak, we ask for your comfort and guidance.

Day 13: Beloved Hekate, on this day we celebrate the joy of friendship and companionship. May your divine light shine upon our friendships, and may we cherish the people in our lives who bring us happiness and support.

Day 14: Hekate, Goddess of love and passion, On this day of hearts and roses, Bless me with the warmth of your fire, Guide me towards true love and desire. May your magic kindle the flame, And bring to me a love that's true and same. Hail Hekate!

Day 15: Hekate, protector of relationships, On this day, I ask for your guidance, May you bless all my connections, And bring harmony to all my intersections. May your presence bring peace and calm, And protect my relationships from all harm. Hail Hekate!

Day 16: Hekate, goddess of magic, we call upon you to help us overcome any obstacles and challenges that may arise in our relationships. We ask for your guidance as we strive towards deeper love, understanding, and harmony with our partners, friends, and family.

Day 17: Hekate, goddess of love, we invoke you to help us be open to love and connection in our relationships. We ask for your guidance as we explore the depths of our emotions and desires, and seek to form meaningful connections with those we care about.

Day 18: Hekate, guide us towards deeper understanding and compassion as we navigate the complexities of our relationships. We ask for your blessings of love, empathy, and intuition as we strive towards deeper connection and intimacy with those we care about.

Day 19: Hekate, goddess of the crossroads, we call upon you to help us recognize the opportunities for growth and transformation in our relationships. We ask for your guidance as we seek to build deeper connections and experience greater levels of love and fulfillment.

Day 20: Hekate, goddess of magic and transformation, we invoke you to help us explore the depths of our emotions and desires in our relationships. We ask for your blessings of love, empathy, and intuition as we navigate the complexities of human connection.

Day 21: Mighty Hekate, we ask that you bless our relationships with your divine healing and transformative power. Help us to release old hurts and negative patterns that may be hindering our ability to give and receive love. Guide us towards greater levels of empathy, compassion, and understanding, and bless us with the strength and courage to communicate with honesty and vulnerability.

Day 22: Hekate, goddess of the underworld, we invoke you to help us confront our fears and shadows as we work towards deeper connection and intimacy in our relationships. We ask for your guidance as we navigate the darker aspects of our own psyche and the psyche of those we care about.

Day 23: Mighty Hekate, we ask that you bless our relationships with your wisdom and guidance. Help us to be present and attentive in our interactions with others, and to communicate with love and empathy. Grant us the strength and courage to be vulnerable and authentic, and bless us with the harmony and balance we need to thrive in our relationships.

Day 24: Hekate, we ask that you bless our relationships with your divine power and protection. Help us to release any negative energies or patterns that may be hindering our ability to give and receive love. Grant us the strength and courage to communicate with love and respect, and bless us with the harmony, balance, and deep connection we need to thrive in our relationships.

Day 25: Mighty Hekate, we ask that you bless our relationships with your wisdom and guidance. Help us to let go of fear and resistance, and to embrace new opportunities for love and connection. Grant us the strength and courage to communicate with honesty and respect, and bless us with the harmony, balance, and deep connection we need to thrive in our relationships.

Day 26: Hekate, we ask that you bless our relationships with your divine power and protection. Help us to release any negative energies or patterns that may be hindering our ability to give and receive love. Guide us towards greater levels of understanding and empathy in our interactions with others, and bless us with the courage and strength to communicate with love and respect. May our relationships be filled with harmony, balance, and deep connection.

Day 27: Mighty Hekate, we ask that you bless our relationships with your wisdom and guidance. Help us to be present and attentive in our interactions with others, and to communicate with love and respect. Grant us the courage to be vulnerable and authentic, and bless us with the harmony, balance, and deep connection we need to thrive in our relationships.

Day 28: Hekate, we ask that you bless our relationships with your divine power and protection. Help us to let go of fear and resistance, and to embrace new opportunities for love and connection. Guide us towards greater levels of empathy and understanding, and bless us with the harmony, balance, and deep connection we need to thrive in our relationships. May our connections with others be filled with love, joy, and fulfillment.

Special Full Moon Ritual for February:

Title: The Blessing of Love and Connection This ritual is designed to enhance and strengthen the loving connections in your life. It is best performed under the light of the full moon.

Materials needed:

- A pink or red candle
- A piece of paper and pen
- Your favorite incense
- A piece of rose quartz
- A bowl of water
- Your Hekate altar

Steps:

1. Begin by lighting your favorite incense and setting the rose quartz in front of you and recite.

"Great Hekate, goddess of love and relationships, we call upon you on this night of the full moon. You who are known for your power to bring people together, to mend broken hearts, and to kindle new flames of passion. You who guide us through the trials and joys of love, and teach us the true meaning of connection.

As we stand under the radiant light of this full moon, we ask for your presence and your blessings. Help us to open our hearts to love, to deepen our existing relationships, and to find new connections that nourish our souls. Grant us the courage to face our fears and our vulnerabilities, and to take the risks necessary for love to flourish.

Hekate, protector and guide, be with us as we journey through the ups and downs of relationships. Help us to communicate with kindness and honesty, to forgive and be forgiven, and to cherish the bonds that sustain us. May your light shine upon us always, and may your love guide us on our path."

2. Sit comfortably and breathe deeply. Focus your energy on your heart chakra and visualize it glowing with pink light.

3. Write down the names of the people you wish to strengthen your connection with. Speak their names out loud and visualize them in front of you.

4. Light the pink or red candle and place it in front of the paper.

5. Close your eyes and invoke Hekate, the goddess of love and connection. Ask her to bless your relationships and fill them with unconditional love and understanding.

6. Hold the rose quartz in your left hand and visualize the energy of love flowing from your heart chakra into the crystal.

7. Dip your right hand into the bowl of water and sprinkle it over the piece of paper with the names of the people you wish to connect with.

8. Recite the following prayer: "Hekate, goddess of love and connection, bless these relationships with your grace. May they be strengthened with love, understanding, and compassion. May our connections be filled with joy and happiness, and may they serve the highest good of all involved. Hail Hekate!"

9. Hold the paper over the flame of the candle and allow it to burn. As the paper burns, visualize the negative energies and obstacles that have hindered your connections being released and transformed into positive energy.

10. Sit in meditation for a few minutes and allow the energy of love and connection to fill you.

11. Close the ritual by thanking Hekate and snuffing out the candle.

Note: This ritual can be performed as often as needed to strengthen the loving connections in your life.

Chapter 4: Prayers for March

March is a collection of sacred invocations and prayers to help you connect with the divine energies of the month of March. In this chapter, you will find powerful invocations and prayers for love, healing, abundance, and transformation, as well as guidance and protection from the wisdom of the universe. These invocations and prayers can be used to enhance your spiritual practice and deepen your connection to the divine.

Day 1: Hekate, goddess of the crossroads, we call upon you to guide us towards growth and transformation. Help us to release the old and welcome the new as we journey forward on our paths. Illuminate our way with your torches and guide us towards the renewal we seek.

Day 2: Hekate, we ask that you bless us with your divine presence and guidance as we journey towards growth and transformation. Help us to see the hidden truths and mysteries of our lives, and to embrace the changes and opportunities for renewal that lie ahead. Protect us from any negative energies or influences that may hinder our progress, and grant us the courage and strength to overcome any obstacles on our path. May your light guide us always.

Day 3: Hekate, guardian of the crossroads, we call upon you to help us make wise decisions as we journey towards growth and transformation. Guide us towards the path that is aligned with our highest good, and help us to release any doubts or fears that may be holding us back. Illuminate the way with your torches and guide us towards the renewal we seek.

Day 4: Hekate, we ask that you bless us with your divine presence and guidance as we seek to connect with our intuition and inner wisdom. Help us to trust in our inner guidance and to navigate the path of growth and transformation with grace and ease. Protect us from any negative energies or influences that may distract us from our true path, and guide us towards the renewal we seek. May your light guide us always.

Day 5: Hekate, goddess of magic, we call upon you to help us tap into the power of the universe as we journey towards growth and transformation. Guide us towards the knowledge and wisdom we need to create the changes we seek in our lives. Illuminate the way with your torches and guide us towards the renewal we seek.

Day 6: Hekate, we ask that you bless us with your wisdom and protection as we release old patterns and beliefs that no longer serve us. Help us to let go of any fears or doubts that may be holding us back from our true potential. Protect us from any negative influences or energies that may hinder our progress, and guide us towards the renewal we seek. May your light guide us always.

Day 7: Hekate, goddess of crossroads, we call upon you to help us find the strength and courage to make positive changes in our lives. As we journey towards growth and transformation, we ask for your guidance and protection on this path. Illuminate the way with your torches and guide us towards the renewal we seek.

Day 8: Hekate, we ask that you bless us with your divine presence and guidance as we seek to connect with the mysteries of the universe. Help us to tap into the wisdom and knowledge that is available to us, and to trust in the guidance of the universe. Protect us from any negative influences or energies that may distract us from our true path, and guide us towards the renewal we seek. May your light guide us always.

Day 9: Hekate, goddess of transitions, we call upon you to help us navigate the changes and transitions in our lives with grace and ease. As we journey towards growth and transformation, we ask for your guidance and protection on this path. Illuminate the way with your torches and guide us towards the renewal we seek.

Day 10: Mighty Hekate, grant me the courage to let go of what no longer serves me and embrace the new opportunities that come my way. May I emerge from this journey stronger and wiser than before.

Day 11: Hekate, Queen of Witches, bless me with your magic and power as I embark on this journey of growth and renewal. Guide me with your torches through the darkness and lead me to the light.

Day 12: Wise Hekate, as I navigate the twists and turns of life, may your guidance light my way. May I embrace the power of renewal and transformation, and emerge from each cycle stronger and wiser than before.

Day 13: Hekate, Goddess of Crossroads, bless me with your guidance and protection as I step into the unknown. May your torches light my way and your magic shield me from harm.

Day 14: Mighty Hekate, as I stand at the crossroads of my life, may your presence surround me and your wisdom guide me. May I find the strength to let go of the past and step into the light of a new dawn.

Day 15: Hekate, Mistress of the Wild, bless me with the power of nature and the magic of the universe. May I grow and transform like the cycles of the moon, and may your guidance light my way through the darkness.

Day16: Mighty Hekate, as I journey through the cycles of life and death, may your wisdom and guidance light my way. May I emerge from this journey transformed, renewed, and strengthened by the power of your magic.

Day 17: Hekate, Queen of Witches, bless me with your power and magic as I journey through the cycles of growth and transformation. May your torches light my way and your spells protect me from harm.

Day 18: Hekate, Guardian of the Crossroads, guide me through the choices and decisions that lie ahead. May your presence be with me as I journey towards growth and transformation.

Day 19: Great Hekate, as I face my fears and doubts, may your magic infuse me with courage and resilience. May I emerge from this journey renewed, transformed, and blessed with the gifts of your wisdom.

Day 20: Hekate, Mistress of the Wild, guide me through the cycles of nature and the magic of the universe. Bless me with the power to grow and transform like the cycles of the moon.

Day March 21: Powerful Hekate, as I journey through the cycles of life and death, may your magic infuse me with vitality and strength. May I emerge from this journey transformed, renewed, and blessed with the gifts of your wisdom and grace.

Day 22: Hekate, Goddess of Renewal, bless me with your magic as I shed old habits and patterns. May your torches light my way and guide me towards growth and transformation.

Day 23: Mighty Hekate, as I face my shadows and embrace the cycles of life and death, may your magic infuse me with courage and strength. May I emerge from this journey transformed, renewed, and blessed with the gifts of your wisdom.

Day 24: Hekate, Queen of Sorcery, bless me with your magic as I embrace the mysteries of transformation and growth. May your spells protect me from harm and guide me towards renewal.

Day 25: Powerful Hekate, as I embrace the cycles of nature and the magic of the universe, may your guidance and protection be my guide. May I emerge from this journey transformed, renewed, and blessed with the gifts of your wisdom and grace.

Day 26: Hekate, Queen of the Crossroads, guide me through the choices and decisions that lie ahead as I seek growth and transformation. May your torches light my way and your magic guide me towards renewal.

Day 27: Hekate, Mistress of the Wild, bless me with your power and magic as I seek growth and transformation. May your presence be with me as I journey towards renewal. Prayer: Wise Hekate, as I embrace the cycles of life and death, may your magic infuse me with vitality and strength. May I emerge from this journey transformed, renewed, and blessed with the gifts of your grace.

Day 28: Great Hekate, as I face the mysteries of life and death, may your power and magic be my strength. May I emerge from this journey transformed, renewed, and blessed with the gifts of your wisdom.

Day 29 Hekate, mistress of the crossroads, I call upon you on this day of endings and beginnings. Grant me the strength to let go of what no longer serves me and embrace the new opportunities that await me.

Day 30: Wise Hekate, I offer my gratitude for your guidance and protection. As I bask in the light of the full moon, may I release all fears and doubts and embrace my true potential. Bless me with your wisdom and help me manifest my deepest desires.

Day 31: Hekate, guardian of the underworld, I call upon you on this day of remembrance. May your strength and compassion help me honor the memories of those who have passed on and find solace in their love and legacy.

Here is the new moon ritual:

Steps:

1. Prepare a sacred space: Set up a clean and peaceful space where you can perform your ritual. Light candles, burn incense, and create an altar with offerings such as flowers, crystals, or herbs.

2. Connect with Hekate: Take a few moments to ground yourself and connect with the energy of the new moon. Close your eyes and visualize a silver light surrounding you, invoking Hekate's presence with the following words:

Hekate, queen of the night and mistress of magic, I invoke your presence on this night of the new moon. May your wisdom and power guide me as I embark on a new journey of growth and transformation.

With this ritual, I ask for your blessings and protection, and invite you to witness my intentions and aspirations.

Great Hekate, mistress of the crossroads and guardian of the night, I call upon you on this new moon night. Come forth and bless this space with your presence. I offer you this altar as a tribute to your wisdom and power. Hear my intentions and guide me towards my highest potential.

3. State your intentions: Take a piece of paper and write down your intentions for the new moon cycle. Be specific and concise, and focus on what you want to achieve or manifest in your life. When you are done, read them out loud, infusing your words with your energy and emotions.

4. Offer your gratitude: Thank Hekate for her presence and blessings, and offer her an offering from your altar. You can also light a candle or burn some incense in her honor.

5. Close the ritual: When you feel ready, release the energy and close the ritual. You can do this by blowing out the candles, taking a few deep breaths, or simply saying "So mote it be."

Hekate, I thank you for your guidance and protection. May your light shine upon me and help me achieve my dreams. Until we meet again, farewell and blessed be!

Chapter 5: Invocations and Prayers for April

As spring begins to blossom, April is a time of renewal and growth. The earth awakens from its winter slumber, and we too can harness this energy to renew our spirits and embrace new opportunities. In this chapter, we offer invocations and prayers to Hekate for guidance, support, and transformation as we navigate the winds of change and emerge into the light of a new season.

Day 1: Hekate, goddess of abundance, I invoke thee. Bless me with your fertile energy and guide me towards prosperity. May my fields be plentiful and my home be filled with abundance. Hail Hekate!

Day 2: Hekate, I call upon thee to open the pathways of wealth and abundance. May my efforts be fruitful and my rewards be bountiful. Help me to attract prosperity and abundance into my life. Hail Hekate!

Day 3: Great Hekate, goddess of the earth and sky, I seek your blessings on this day. Bless me with the energy of growth and fertility, and guide me towards abundance and prosperity. Hail Hekate!

Day 4: Hekate, goddess of the crossroads, hear my prayer. Guide me towards the paths of prosperity and abundance. May my life be filled with blessings, and may my efforts be rewarded. Hail Hekate!

Day 5: Hekate, goddess of the moon and stars, I invoke thee. Fill my life with abundance and prosperity, and help me to manifest my goals and dreams. May your blessings be upon me always. Hail Hekate!

Day 6: Great Hekate, goddess of fertility and growth, I seek your blessings on this day. Bless my fields, bless my home, and bless my life with abundance and prosperity. May your energy guide me towards success. Hail Hekate!

Day 7: Hekate, goddess of the wild and free, I call upon thee. Help me to break free from limitations and embrace abundance and prosperity. Guide me towards success and fulfillment, and may your blessings be upon me always. Hail Hekate!

Day 8: Hekate, goddess of the dark moon, I invoke thee. Help me to release any blockages or limitations to my abundance and prosperity. May my life be filled with blessings and abundance, and may your energy guide me towards success. Hail Hekate!

Day 9: Great Hekate, goddess of the underworld, hear my prayer. Bless me with your fertile energy and guide me towards abundance and prosperity. May my efforts be fruitful and my rewards be bountiful. Hail Hekate!

Day 10: Hekate, goddess of the crossroads, I call upon thee. Bless my life with abundance and prosperity, and guide me towards the paths of success. May your energy guide me towards fulfillment and happiness. Hail Hekate!

Day 11: Hekate, goddess of the moon and stars, hear my prayer. Bless me with the energy of abundance and prosperity, and guide me towards success in all areas of my life. May your blessings be upon me always. Hail Hekate!

Day 12: Great Hekate, goddess of the earth and sky, I invoke thee. Bless my life with abundance and prosperity, and guide me towards the paths of success. May your energy be with me always. Hail Hekate!

Day 13: Hekate, goddess of the wild and free, I call upon thee. Help me to embrace abundance and prosperity, and guide me towards the fulfillment of my dreams. May your blessings be upon me always. Hail Hekate!

Day 14: Great Hekate, goddess of the dark moon, hear my prayer. Help me to release any blockages to my abundance and prosperity, and guide me towards success and fulfillment. May your energy guide me towards the paths of happiness and joy. Hail Hekate!

Day 15: Hekate, goddess of abundance and prosperity, Bless me with your favor and help me to create wealth, May my financial situation improve and my bank account grow, May I always have enough to support myself and those I love.

Day 16: Hekate, bringer of fertility and growth, I ask for your blessings on my endeavors, May my creative projects flourish and my dreams come to life, May my efforts be fruitful and my success abundant.

Day 17: Hekate, goddess of the earth and its riches, Bless my home with your abundance and prosperity, May my household be filled with love, happiness, and financial stability, May our needs be met and our desires fulfilled.

Day 18: Hekate, queen of the underworld and the unseen, Bless me with your wisdom and guidance, Help me to make wise financial decisions and to attract abundance, May I always be prosperous in all aspects of my life.

Day 19: Hekate, goddess of the crossroads, Guide me towards financial prosperity and abundance, May I always be aware of the opportunities and resources available to me, May I be successful in all my endeavors and live a life of abundance.

Day 20: Hekate, mistress of the night, Bless my dreams and my visions, May my creative ideas be transformed into successful endeavors, May my financial situation improve and my abundance increase.

Day 21: Hekate, goddess of the moon and the tides, Bless my financial situation with your abundance and prosperity, May my wealth grow and my resources increase, May I always have enough to support myself and those I love.

Day 22: Hekate, goddess of the harvest and the seasons, Bless me with your abundance and prosperity, May I reap the rewards of my hard work and dedication, May my financial situation improve and my wealth grow.

Day 23: Hekate, guardian of the gates, Open the doors of financial opportunity and abundance for me, May I always be aware of the resources available to me, May my financial situation improve and my prosperity increase.

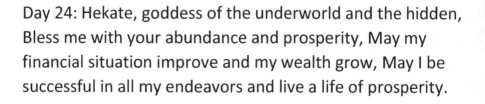

Day 24: Hekate, goddess of the underworld and the hidden, Bless me with your abundance and prosperity, May my financial situation improve and my wealth grow, May I be successful in all my endeavors and live a life of prosperity.

Day 25: Hekate, goddess of the crossroads, Guide me towards financial success and abundance, May I always be aware of the opportunities available to me, May my resources increase and my wealth grow.

Day 26: Hekate, queen of the night and the unseen, Bless me with your wisdom and guidance, Help me to make wise financial decisions and to attract abundance, May my financial situation improve and my wealth grow.

Day 27: Hekate, goddess of the moon and the stars, Bless me with your abundance and prosperity, May my financial situation improve and my resources increase, May I always have enough to support myself and those I love.

Day 28: Hekate, mistress of the crossroads, Guide me towards financial success and abundance, May I be aware of the opportunities available to me, May my resources increase and my wealth grow.

Day 29: Hekate, goddess of the underworld and the unseen, Bless me with your wisdom and guidance, Help me to make wise financial decisions and to attract abundance, May my financial situation improve and my prosperity increase.

Day 30: Hekate, ancient goddess of magic and power, I call upon you on this day to ask for your blessings of abundance and fertility. You who hold the power of the moon, bring forth the energy of growth and expansion into my life. May I be filled with abundance and prosperity, and may I experience the joys of fertility in all areas of my life.

New Moon Ritual for April

This ritual is designed to honor Hekate, goddess of magic, the crossroads, and the moon, during the new moon in April. This is a time of new beginnings, growth, and fertility.

You will need:

- A black or silver candle
- A small bowl of salt
- A small bowl of water
- Myrrh or frankincense incense
- A piece of paper and a pen
- Any other offerings you wish to make to Hekate (e.g. flowers, crystals, etc.)

Instructions:

1. Find a quiet, dark place where you will not be disturbed. Set up your altar by placing the candle, bowls of salt and water, and incense on a table or other flat surface. Arrange any other offerings you wish to make to Hekate around the altar.

2. Light the incense and take a moment to ground and center yourself. Take a few deep breaths and focus on your intention for this ritual.

3. Light the candle and say the following invocation to Hekate:

"Great Hekate, goddess of magic, the crossroads, and the moon, I call upon you now to honor and invoke your divine presence. With this candle, I light the way for your guidance and protection. May your light illuminate my path and lead me towards growth and prosperity. Hail Hekate!"

4. Take the piece of paper and write down your intention for this new moon cycle. Be specific and clear in your intentions. Once you have written it down, hold the paper over the flame of the candle and let it burn. As it burns, visualize your intention manifesting in your life.

5. Dip your fingers in the bowl of salt and sprinkle it around the candle, while saying:

"With this salt, I purify and protect my sacred space. May no harm come to me or my intention, and may Hekate's energy surround and bless me."

6. Dip your fingers in the bowl of water and sprinkle it around the candle, while saying:

"With this water, I bless and consecrate my sacred space. May the energy of Hekate flow through me and guide me towards growth and prosperity."

7. Spend a few moments in meditation, focusing on your intention and allowing Hekate's energy to flow through you.

8. When you are ready, thank Hekate for her guidance and protection. Extinguish the candle and clean up your altar.

May the energy of Hekate guide you towards growth, prosperity, and new beginnings during this new moon cycle. Hail Hekate!

Chapter 6: Prayers for May.

As the days grow longer and warmer, May is a time of beauty, creativity, and inspiration. Whether you are seeking abundance in your personal or professional life, looking to deepen your spiritual practice, or simply wishing to connect with the energies of the season, the invocations and prayers in this chapter can be a powerful tool. May they inspire and uplift you, as you journey through this magical time of year.

Day 1: Hekate, goddess of magic and inspiration, I call upon you to bless me with the creative energy and inspiration I need to bring my visions to life. Grant me the courage to explore new paths and the patience to see my projects through to completion.

Day 2: Hekate, guardian of the crossroads, guide me as I embark on new creative endeavors. Help me to tap into my inner wisdom and find new ways to express myself through art, music, or writing.

Day 3: Hekate, goddess of the moon, I ask for your blessings on my creative process. May your cycles of waxing and waning inspire me to grow and evolve in my artistic pursuits.

Day 4: Hekate, goddess of beauty, I ask for your blessings on my physical appearance. May I see the beauty in myself and others, and may I be surrounded by positive energy and affirmations.

Day 5: Hekate, goddess of transformation, I ask for your guidance as I seek to reinvent myself. Help me to embrace change and find the strength to let go of what no longer serves me.

Day 6: Hekate, goddess of the wilderness, I ask for your blessings on my connection to nature. May I find inspiration in the beauty of the natural world and may I be a caretaker and protector of the earth.

Day 7: Hekate, goddess of the night, I call upon you to help me embrace the darkness within myself. May I find healing and transformation in the shadows, and may I learn to see the beauty in the unknown.

Day 8: Hekate, goddess of the underworld, I ask for your blessings on my journey through the depths of my psyche. May I find strength in the face of adversity and emerge from the darkness with a renewed sense of purpose.

Day 9: Hekate, goddess of magic, I ask for your guidance as I seek to deepen my spiritual practice. May I find new ways to connect with the divine and may my rituals and offerings be received with love and gratitude.

Day 10: Hekate, goddess of crossroads, I ask for your guidance as I navigate new paths in my life. May I have the courage to choose wisely and the humility to ask for help when I need it.

Day 11: Hekate, goddess of witchcraft, I call upon you to bless my magickal workings. May my spells and rituals be imbued with your power and may I use them only for good.

Day 12: Hekate, goddess of the sea, I ask for your blessings on my emotional wellbeing. May I learn to ride the waves of my feelings and find peace in the ebb and flow of life.

Day 13: Hekate, goddess of the wild hunt, I ask for your blessings on my journey through life. May I embrace the adventure and the challenges, and may I find joy in the journey itself.

Day 14: Hekate, goddess of the mist, I call upon you to help me see through the veil of illusion. May I have the clarity and discernment to see the truth and the wisdom to act upon it.

Day 15: Hekate, goddess of the torches, I ask for your blessings on my journey through the dark. May your light guide me through the shadows and illuminate my path ahead.

Day 16: Hekate, guide me towards the beauty within and around me. Help me to see the wonders in nature and to appreciate the little things in life. Bless me with a creative spirit and inspire me to create art that reflects the beauty of the world.

Day 17: Hekate, goddess of the night, fill me with your divine inspiration. Help me to tap into my inner wisdom and creativity so that I may express myself fully and authentically. Guide me towards the path of my highest purpose.

Day 18: Hekate, goddess of the crossroads, I ask for your guidance as I make important decisions. Help me to see all the options before me and to choose the path that is aligned with my highest good. Fill me with the courage and confidence to follow my heart.

Day 19: Hekate, goddess of magic and transformation, I ask for your blessings on my creative projects. Infuse them with your magic and help them to manifest into physical form. May they bring beauty and joy to the world.

Day 20: Hekate, goddess of the moon, bless me with your feminine energy and intuition. Help me to connect with the cycles of the moon and to honor the natural rhythms of life. Guide me towards inner peace and harmony.

Day 21: Hekate, goddess of witchcraft and sorcery, I ask for your wisdom and guidance as I explore the mysteries of the universe. Help me to deepen my understanding of magic and to use my powers for the highest good.

Day 22: Hekate, goddess of the underworld, guide me through the darkness of my inner world. Help me to confront my fears and to release what no longer serves me. Bless me with the strength and resilience to face any challenge.

Day 23: Hekate, goddess of the crossroads, I ask for your guidance as I navigate the choices before me. Help me to make decisions that align with my highest good and to stay true to my values and purpose.

Day 24: Hekate, goddess of the night, I ask for your protection and guidance as I venture into the unknown. Help me to overcome my fears and to trust in the journey ahead. Bless me with your wisdom and insight.

Day 25: Hekate, goddess of the moon, I honor you and your ever-changing phases. Help me to connect with the magic of the moon and to use its energy to manifest my desires. Guide me towards my highest destiny.

Day 26: Hekate, goddess of witchcraft and sorcery, I call upon you to help me access my own magical powers. Infuse me with your energy and wisdom so that I may cast spells and perform rituals that align with my highest good.

Day 27: Hekate, goddess of the underworld, I ask for your guidance as I journey into the depths of my soul. Help me to release what no longer serves me and to embrace the transformative power of change. Bless me with the courage to face my shadows.

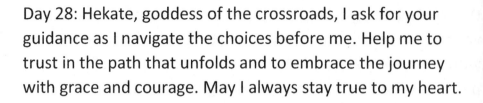

Day 28: Hekate, goddess of the crossroads, I ask for your guidance as I navigate the choices before me. Help me to trust in the path that unfolds and to embrace the journey with grace and courage. May I always stay true to my heart.

Day 29: Hekate, goddess of the night, I honor you and your sacred mysteries. Help me to connect with the unseen realms and to access the wisdom of the ages. Bless me with your guidance and protection.

Day 30: Hail Hekate, goddess of beauty and inspiration, I call upon you to bless this day with your divine energy. May your divine inspiration and passion guide me towards creating art that reveals the beauty and majesty of nature.

Day 31: Hekate, divine goddess of inspiration, I call upon you on this final day of May to help me tap into the wellspring of creativity within me. May your fire ignite my passion and fuel my imagination, so that I may bring forth my most inspired creations into the world. Help me to see the beauty in all things, and to find the inspiration in the mundane. With your guidance, may I continue to cultivate my creative gifts and share them with the world. Hail Hekate!

Special new moon ritual for May, invoking Hekate

You will need:

- A black candle
- A white candle
- A small bowl of water
- A small bowl of salt
- An offering of your choice (such as herbs, crystals, or flowers)
- A piece of paper and pen

Instructions:

1. Begin by cleansing yourself and your space with the bowl of water and salt. Sprinkle the salt into the water and use your hands to splash the mixture over your body and around the room.

2. Light the black candle and say the following invocation: "Hekate, queen of the night and goddess of the crossroads, I call upon you to join me in this sacred space. May your light guide me through the darkness and bring me closer to your divine wisdom and power."

3. Take a few deep breaths and meditate on your intentions for the month ahead. Focus on the areas of your life where you seek growth and change, and how Hekate's energy can support you in these endeavors.

4. Write your intentions on the piece of paper, and offer it to Hekate by burning it in the flame of the black candle.

5. Light the white candle and say the following prayer: "Hekate, goddess of magic and transformation, I offer you this white light as a symbol of my faith and devotion. May it illuminate my path and guide me towards my highest purpose."

6. Place your offering in front of the white candle, and meditate on your gratitude for Hekate's presence in your life. Take a few moments to thank her for her blessings, and ask for her continued support and guidance in the days and weeks ahead.

7. When you feel ready, blow out the candles and offer your thanks once more to Hekate for her presence and blessings.

8. Dispose of the ashes and any remnants of the ritual in a respectful and mindful way, such as burying them in the earth or scattering them in a body of water.

Closing Invocation: "Hekate, goddess of the new moon, I thank you for your presence and guidance in this sacred space. May your wisdom and power continue to guide me on my journey towards spiritual growth and transformation. Hail Hekate!"

Chapter 7: Prayers for June

In this chapter, the focus is on healing, health, and well-being. Hekate is a goddess who has been revered for thousands of years for her ability to heal both physical and emotional ailments. Her guidance and blessings can bring about transformation and renewal, leading to a healthier and happier life.

Whether you are struggling with physical illness, mental health challenges, or simply seeking to improve your overall well-being, the prayers to Hekate in this chapter offer a powerful source of healing and support. Join us as we delve into the rich history and mythology surrounding Hekate, and discover the transformative power of her healing energies.

Day 1: Hail Hekate, goddess of healing and well-being, I call upon you to bless this day with your divine energy. May your healing light and transformative power guide me towards greater physical, mental, and emotional health.

Day 2: Hekate, goddess of medicine and healing, I offer this prayer to you. May your sacred energy infuse my body and mind with healing light and strength, and may I be open to receiving your blessings of health and vitality.

Day 3: Hail Hekate, goddess of the night and the healer of the soul, I call upon you to bless this day with your divine energy. May your transformative power and wisdom guide me towards greater emotional and spiritual well-being.

Day 4: Hekate, goddess of medicine and the mind, I offer this prayer to you. May your sacred energy infuse my thoughts and emotions with healing light and strength, and may I be open to receiving your blessings of mental and emotional health.

Day 5: Hail Hekate, goddess of the body and the healer of the physical, I call upon you to bless this day with your divine energy. May your transformative power and wisdom guide me towards greater physical health and well-being.

Day 6: Hekate, mistress of the flames of transformation, I offer this prayer to you. May your sacred energy infuse my heart and soul with healing light and strength, and may I be open to receiving your blessings of emotional and spiritual health.

Day 7: Hail Hekate, goddess of the healing waters, I call upon you to bless my body and mind with your divine energy. May your transformative power and wisdom guide me towards greater physical and mental well-being.

Day 8: Hekate, mistress of the earth and the healing soil, I offer this prayer to you. May your sacred energy infuse my connection with the earth and physical body with healing light and strength, and may I be open to receiving your blessings of physical health and vitality.

Day 9: Hail Hekate, goddess of the healing winds, I call upon you to bless my mind and spirit with your divine energy. May your transformative power and wisdom guide me towards greater mental and spiritual well-being.

Day 10: Hekate, mistress of the healing light and the transformational flame, I offer this prayer to you. May your sacred energy infuse my entire being with healing light and strength, and may I be open to receiving your blessings of health and well-being in all aspects of my life.

Day 11: Hekate, goddess of the crossroads, I call upon you to bless this day with your presence. Guide me on my path towards healing, and help me find the strength and courage to overcome any obstacles in my way.

Day 12: Hekate, mistress of the moon and the stars, I offer this prayer to you. May your light wash over me, illuminating the darkness and filling me with hope and renewed energy. Help me to let go of any pain or suffering, and open myself up to the healing power of your divine presence.

Day 13: Hekate, goddess of magic and mystery, I call upon you to bless this day with your transformative energy. May your magic help me to release old patterns and habits, and embrace new practices that support my health and well-being.

Day 14: Hekate, goddess of the earth and the underworld, I call upon you to bless this day with your grounding energy. May your connection to the earth help me to find stability and balance in my physical body, and may your wisdom guide me towards practices that support my overall well-being.

Day 15: Hekate, mistress of the crossroads and guide of the sick, I offer this prayer to you. May your transformative power guide me towards choices that support my healing journey, and give me the courage and strength to release those that do not. Help me to stay focused on my path towards greater health and well-being, and to trust in your divine guidance.

Day 16: Hekate, goddess of the moon and the stars, I call upon you to bless this day with your luminous energy. May your light shine upon my path, illuminating the way forward and filling me with hope and inspiration.

Day 17: Hekate, mistress of magic and mystery, I offer this prayer to you. May your transformative power help me to release any limiting beliefs or self-doubt that may be blocking my path towards healing, and empower me to embrace my full potential. Guide me towards practices that support my physical, mental, emotional, and spiritual well-being, and help me to stay aligned with your divine will.

Day 18: Hekate, goddess of the earth and the underworld, I call upon you to bless this day with your grounding energy. Help me to stay centered and focused on my healing journey, and guide me towards practices that support my overall well-being.

Day 19: Hekate, mistress of the crossroads and guide of the sick, I offer this prayer to you. May your transformative power guide me towards choices that support my healing journey, and give me the courage and strength to release those that do not. Help me to stay focused on my path towards greater health and well-being, and to trust in your divine guidance.

Day 20: Hekate, goddess of the moon and the stars, I call upon you to bless this day with your luminous energy. May your light illuminate my path and guide me towards greater health and well-being, and may your wisdom help me to make the right choices and decisions along the way.

Day 21: Hekate, mistress of the night and the underworld, I offer this prayer to you. May your transformative power help me to release any fears, doubts, or anxieties that may be blocking my path towards healing, and guide me towards a place of inner peace and harmony. Help me to trust in your divine guidance, and to stay connected to your sacred energy throughout my healing journey.

Day 22: Hekate, goddess of the wilderness and the wild places, I call upon you to bless this day with your untamed energy. May your wildness inspire me to explore new practices and ways of being that support my physical, mental, emotional, and spiritual well-being, and guide me towards greater health and vitality.

Day 23: Hekate, goddess of magic and transformation, I offer this prayer to you. May your transformative power work within me to heal any wounds that I may carry, and guide me towards greater health and well-being. Help me to trust in the magic of the universe, and to have faith in my ability to transform and heal.

Day 24: Hekate, goddess of the moon and the night, I call upon you to bless this day with your soothing energy. May your calming presence ease any anxiety or stress that I may be feeling, and help me to find peace and restful sleep.

Day 25: Hekate, goddess of the underworld and the dead, I offer this prayer to you. May your transformative energy help me to release any old patterns or beliefs that are holding me back, and guide me towards new growth and healing. Help me to trust in the transformative power of death and rebirth, and to embrace change with open arms.

Day 26: Hekate, goddess of the crossroads and the liminal spaces, I call upon you to bless this day with your guidance. May your wisdom and insight help me to navigate any challenges or decisions that I may face, and guide me towards the path that leads to greater health and well-being.

Day 27: Hekate, goddess of the wilderness and the wild places, I offer this prayer to you. May your untamed energy inspire me to connect with the natural world and find healing and renewal in its beauty. Help me to trust in the wisdom of nature, and to find peace and healing in its wildness.

Day 28: Hekate, goddess of the torches and the light-bringer, I call upon you to bless this day with your illuminating energy. May your light guide me towards greater clarity and insight, and help me to see the path that leads to health and well-being.

Day 29: Hekate, goddess of the crossroads and the liminal spaces, I offer this prayer to you. May your transformative energy help me to release any fears or doubts that are holding me back, and guide me towards new growth and healing. Help me to trust in the transformative power of the liminal spaces, and to embrace change with open arms.

Day 30: Hekate, goddess of magic and mystery, I call upon you to bless this day with your enchanting energy. May your mystical presence awaken my senses and fill me with wonder and awe, and help me to see the world with fresh eyes.

Here is the June new moon ritual

Materials:

- A white candle
- A piece of paper and pen
- A bowl of water
- Incense (optional)

Instructions:

1. Find a quiet and comfortable space to perform the ritual. Light the white candle and any incense if you have it.

2. Sit or stand in front of the candle and take a few deep breaths to center yourself.

3. Begin by invoking Hekate with the following words:

"Hekate, great goddess of the night, I call upon you to join me in this rite. Your healing touch and wisdom I seek, As I honor you on this night so meek. Hear my call and bless this space, And guide me towards health and grace."

4. Take a moment to connect with Hekate's energy, and visualize her presence surrounding you.

5. Take the piece of paper and write down any physical, emotional, or spiritual issues that you would like Hekate's help with.

6. Hold the paper over the bowl of water and say the following:

"Hekate, goddess of the threefold way, I offer these troubles to you this day. Bless this water with your healing might, And wash away all that is not right."

7. Place the paper into the bowl of water and let it soak for a few minutes, allowing Hekate's energy to infuse the water.

8. Take the bowl of water and pour it over your hands or face, imagining the water washing away any negative energy or illness.

9. Take a moment to thank Hekate for her presence and blessings, and blow out the candle to end the ritual.

May Hekate's healing energy guide you towards greater health and well-being.

Chapter 8: Invocations and Prayers for July

As we continue our journey with Hekate, we turn our attention to the month of July, a time when many of us seek protection, safety, and security in our daily lives. Hekate, as the guardian of the crossroads and the protectress of all those who call upon her, is a powerful ally in times of danger or uncertainty.

In this chapter, we offer invocations and prayers to Hekate that focus on invoking her protective energy, helping us to feel secure and supported as we navigate the challenges of life. May her powerful presence guide us towards safety and security, and may we find peace and protection in her loving embrace.

Day 1: Hekate, guardian of the crossroads and protectress of all who call upon you, I call upon you to bless this day with your protective energy. May your watchful gaze keep me safe and secure as I move through the world.

Day 2: Hekate, mistress of the night and queen of the shadows, I offer this prayer to you. May your fierce energy guide me towards greater safety and security as I face the challenges of the day. Help me to trust in your ability to lead me through the darkness, and to emerge stronger and more resilient on the other side.

Day 3: Hekate, goddess of the wilderness and the wild places, I call upon you to bless this day with your untamed energy. May your power to survive and thrive in the untamed world help me to feel safe and secure as I explore new paths.

Day 4: Hekate, goddess of magic and mystery, I offer this prayer to you. May your enchanting energy help me to feel safe and secure in the face of the unknown, and to embrace the mysteries of life with open arms. Help me to trust in the magic of the universe, and to have faith in the guidance that you provide.

Day 5: Hekate, mistress of the keys and guardian of the threshold, I call upon you to bless this day with your protective energy. May your power to guard the gates and keep out unwanted energies help me to feel safe and secure in my home and in my heart.

Day 6: Hekate, goddess of the moon and ruler of the tides, I offer this prayer to you. May your fluid energy help me to feel safe and secure in the face of change, and to trust in the natural ebb and flow of life. Help me to surrender to the movement of the universe, and to have faith in the path that you have laid out for me.

Day 7: Hekate, queen of witches and mistress of magic, I call upon you to bless this day with your powerful energy. May your magic protect me and keep me safe as I walk my path.

Day 8: Hekate, goddess of the night and protector of travelers, I offer this prayer to you. May your watchful eye guide me and protect me on my journeys, both physical and spiritual, and help me to feel safe and secure as I explore new horizons. Help me to trust in your guidance, and to have faith in the strength and resilience that you provide.

Day 9: Hekate, goddess of the underworld and guide of the dead, I call upon you to bless this day with your transformative energy. May your power to transform and renew help me to feel safe and secure in the face of endings and beginnings.

Day 10: Hekate, goddess of the crossroads and keeper of the keys, I offer this prayer to you. May your protective energy guard the gates and keep out unwanted energies, both in my boundaries and in my relationships. Help me to trust in your power to keep me safe and secure, and to feel the strength of your loving embrace.

Day 11: Hekate, goddess of the dark moon and bringer of shadows, I call upon you to bless this day with your empowering energy. May your power to embrace the shadow self help me to feel safe and secure in my own authenticity and power.

Day 12: Hekate, goddess of the hunt and protector of wildlife, I offer this prayer to you. May your fierce energy help me to feel safe and secure in my own inner wilderness, and to protect and defend the wild places within me. Help me to trust in the untamed power of the universe, and to feel the strength of your loving guidance.

Day 13: Hekate, goddess of the moon and keeper of secrets, I call upon you to bless this day with your mysterious energy. May your power to hold secrets and mysteries help me to feel safe and secure in my own inner knowledge and intuition.

Day 14: Hekate, goddess of fire and keeper of the hearth, I call upon you to bless this day with your nurturing energy. May your power to warm and protect the home help me to feel safe and secure in my own space.

Day 15: Hekate, goddess of the sea and mistress of storms, I offer this prayer to you. May your elemental energy calm the waters and guide the winds, and help me to feel safe and secure in the face of chaos and change. Help me to trust in the natural ebb and flow of life, and to feel the strength of your loving embrace.

Day 16: Hekate, goddess of the dawn and bringer of light, I call upon you to bless this day with your illuminating energy. May your power to bring clarity and insight help me to feel safe and secure in my own inner wisdom and truth.

Day 17: Hekate, goddess of the earth and guardian of nature, I offer this prayer to you. May your grounding energy connect me to the natural world, and help me to feel safe and secure in my own physical body and in the world around me. Help me to cultivate a sense of rootedness and stability, and to feel the strength of your loving presence.

Day 18: Hekate, goddess of the sky and bringer of rain, I call upon you to bless this day with your cleansing energy. May your power to purify and refresh help me to feel safe and secure in my own emotional and spiritual well-being.

Day 19: Hekate, goddess of the crossroads and guide of souls, I offer this prayer to you. May your guiding energy help me to navigate the unknown and the unfamiliar, and help me to feel safe and secure as I journey through life. Help me to trust in the path that you have laid out for me, and to feel the strength of your loving presence.

Day 20: Hekate, goddess of magic and keeper of the keys, I call upon you to bless this day with your mystical energy. May your power to unlock hidden doors and reveal hidden truths help me to feel safe and secure in the mystery of life.

Day 21: Hekate, goddess of the underworld and guardian of the dead, I offer this prayer to you. May your protective energy guard the realm of the dead and protect the souls of the departed, and help me to feel safe and secure in the afterlife. Help me to trust in the cycle of life and death, and to feel the strength of your loving presence.

Day 22: Hekate, goddess of the night and queen of the witches, I call upon you to bless this day with your magical energy. May your power to connect me to the unseen world and the energies of the universe help me to feel safe and secure in my own power and magic.

Day 23: Hekate, goddess of the hunt and protector of the wild, I offer this prayer to you. May your fierce energy protect and defend the wild places, and help me to feel safe and secure in my own fierceness and strength. Help me to embrace my own wild nature, and to feel the strength of your loving presence.

Day 24: Hekate, goddess of the moon and mistress of the tides, I call upon you to bless this day with your powerful energy. May your power to control the tides and the ebbs and flows of life help me to feel safe and secure in the natural cycles of the universe.

Day 25: Hekate, goddess of the hearth and home, I offer this prayer to you. May your nurturing energy protect and provide for the home and family, and help me to feel safe and secure in the warmth of my own hearth. Help me to create a loving and supportive home environment, and to feel the strength of your loving presence.

Day 26: Hekate, goddess of the liminal spaces and the in-between, I call upon you to bless this day with your transformative energy. May your power to navigate the boundaries and thresholds help me to feel safe and secure as I move through the transitions of life.

Day 27: Hekate, goddess of the crossroads and the choices we make, I offer this prayer to you. May your wise energy guide me towards the right path and the right choices, and help me to feel safe and secure in my own decision-making process. Help me to trust in my own intuition and inner wisdom, and to feel the strength of your loving presence.

Day 28: Hekate, goddess of the night and the mysteries of the universe, I call upon you to bless this day with your deep energy. May your power to penetrate the mysteries of the universe and reveal hidden truths help me to feel safe and secure in the depths of my own soul.

Day 29: Hekate, goddess of the underworld and the afterlife, I call upon you to bless this day with your transformative energy. May your power to guide souls through the afterlife and bring them to new beginnings help me to feel safe and secure in the face of death and rebirth.

Day 30: Hekate, goddess of the triple crossroads, I offer this prayer to you. May your triple form protect me from harm, and your powerful energy keep me safe and secure in all aspects of my life. Help me to navigate the crossroads of life with ease, and to feel the strength of your loving presence.

Special New Moon ritual for July

Items needed:

- A candle (black or silver)
- Frankincense or myrrh incense
- A piece of paper and pen
- A small bowl of water

Steps:

1. Find a quiet, comfortable space where you will not be disturbed. Light the candle and the incense.

2. Take a few deep breaths, and focus on the flame of the candle. Visualize it as a symbol of Hekate's protective energy surrounding you.

3. Write down on the piece of paper any fears or concerns you have about your safety or security. These can be physical, emotional, or spiritual.

4. Hold the paper over the candle flame, and allow it to burn. As it burns, visualize the flames purifying your fears and concerns, and releasing them into the universe.

5. Dip your fingers into the bowl of water, and sprinkle it around the candle and the area around you. As you do this, visualize the water washing away any negative energy and replacing it with Hekate's protective energy.

6. Close your eyes and invoke Hekate:

"Great Hekate, goddess of the crossroads, keeper of the keys, hear my call. On this new moon night, I ask for your presence and protection. Mighty goddess, guide me through the darkness, and lend me your strength and wisdom. I call upon you, Hekate, to bless this ritual and to protect me from all harm."

7. Sit in silence for a few moments, and allow yourself to feel Hekate's presence and protection.

8. When you are ready, blow out the candle and thank Hekate for her guidance and protection. Keep the piece of burnt paper as a reminder of the fears and concerns you released during the ritual, and the protection you received from Hekate.

Chapter 9: Invocations and Prayers for August

As we enter the month of August, we are reminded of the power and intensity of the summer season. This is a time when we may face challenges that require us to tap into our inner strength and courage. In this chapter, we will call upon Hekate, the goddess of the crossroads, to guide us on our journey towards greater strength, courage, and perseverance. Through these invocations and prayers, we will connect with Hekate's powerful energy and draw upon her wisdom to navigate the challenges that lie ahead. Let us open our hearts and minds to the guidance of Hekate, and embrace the strength and courage that lies within us all.

Day 1: Mighty Hekate, goddess of the crossroads and guide through the unknown, I call upon your strength and wisdom to lead me through the challenges that lie ahead. Fill me with the courage and determination I need to persevere, and grant me the power to overcome any obstacle in my path.

Day 2: Hekate, mistress of the night, I offer this prayer to you. Grant me the strength and courage to navigate the unseen world with grace and determination. Help me to trust in my intuition and inner wisdom, and to draw upon your powerful guidance to overcome any obstacle in my path. Bless me with your protection and steadfast support.

Day 3: Mighty Hekate, goddess of the crossroads and guardian of the keys, I call upon your strength and courage to unlock the doors to my inner power and resilience. Empower me to face the challenges of this day with confidence and determination, and to persevere in the face of adversity.

Day 4: Hekate, guide through the unknown, I offer this prayer to you. Grant me the strength and courage to face the challenges of this day with grace and perseverance. Help me to tap into my inner wisdom and power, and to draw upon your guidance and support to overcome any obstacle in my path. Bless me with your protection and steadfast presence.

Day 5: Hekate, mistress of the night, I offer this prayer to you. Bless me with the strength and courage to navigate the challenges of this day with grace and resilience. Help me to trust in my inner wisdom and power, and to draw upon your guidance and protection to overcome any obstacle in my path. Guide me on my journey, and protect me with your mighty energy.

Day 6: Hekate, guardian of the crossroads, I call upon you to lend me your strength and courage as I navigate the challenges of this day. Help me to stay focused and determined in the face of adversity, and guide me towards success and victory.

Day 7: Hekate, divine goddess of the moon and the night sky, I offer this prayer to you. May your light shine bright and guide me towards my dreams, and may I have the courage and strength to pursue them with all my heart. Help me to stay focused on my path, even when the way seems dark and uncertain.

Day 8: Hekate, queen of witches, I call upon you to empower me with your strength and courage as I undertake my magical work. May your wisdom guide me as I weave spells and perform rituals, and may your protection keep me safe from harm.

Day 9: Hekate, mistress of the wilderness and the untamed places, I offer this prayer to you. Grant me the strength and courage I need to explore the unknown, and fill me with your wildness and fearlessness. Keep me safe on my journey with your powerful protection, and guide me towards the path that leads to my highest good.

Day 10: Hekate, goddess of transformation and change, I call upon you to grant me the strength and courage to embrace new beginnings. May your wisdom guide me as I navigate the twists and turns of life, and may your protection keep me safe as I venture forth into the unknown.

Day 11: Hekate, guide me on my journey and give me the strength to overcome obstacles. May I have the courage to face the challenges ahead and the perseverance to keep going, even when the path is difficult. Your crossroads offer me choices and opportunities for growth, and I trust in your guidance to choose the path that is right for me.

Day 12: Hekate, guardian of the night, I call upon your protection and strength on this day. As I face the darkness and the unknown, may your light guide me and your strength protect me. Grant me the courage to face my fears and the perseverance to overcome them.

Day 13: Hekate, goddess of magic, I ask for your power and wisdom. Grant me the strength to harness my own magic and the courage to use it wisely. May your wisdom guide me as I explore the mysteries of the universe and the depths of my own soul. Help me to use my magic to create positive change in my life and in the world around me.

Day 14: Hekate, goddess of the underworld, I call upon your strength and guidance on this day. As I journey through the depths of my own psyche, may your wisdom and guidance be my light. Grant me the courage to face the shadows within me and the perseverance to heal and transform.

Day 15: Hekate, queen of witches, I ask for your power and wisdom. As a fellow witch, I seek your guidance and inspiration to deepen my practice and strengthen my connection to the divine. Grant me the courage to trust in my own intuition and the perseverance to continue on this path, even when it is challenging. May my practice honor you and bring positive change to my life and the world around me.

Day 16: Hekate, goddess of the crossroads and the liminal spaces, I call upon you to bless this day with your guidance and protection. May your presence help me navigate the challenges that lie ahead and give me the strength to persevere.

Day 17: Hekate, mistress of magic and transformation, I offer this prayer to you. May your magic fill me with strength, courage, and perseverance. Help me transform any negativity in my life into positivity and growth. Thank you for your powerful blessings.

Day 18: Hekate, goddess of the night and the shadows, I call upon you to bless this day with your wisdom and insight. May your presence help me see through the darkness and find the light that shines within me.

Day 19: Hekate, mistress of the sea and the storms, I offer this prayer to you. May your power and protection surround me and keep me safe from harm. Help me weather any storms that come my way and give me the strength to overcome any obstacles. Thank you for your steadfast presence.

Day 20: Hekate, goddess of the wilderness and the untamed places, I call upon you to bless this day with your wild energy and strength. May your untamed spirit infuse me with courage and vitality.

Day 21: Hekate, mistress of the moon and the cycles of life, I offer this prayer to you. May your cycles of change and transformation help me embrace the ups and downs of life. Give me the strength to persevere through difficult times and the courage to embrace new beginnings. Thank you for your guiding presence.

Day 22: Hekate, powerful queen of the night, I call upon you to bless me with your strength and courage. As I navigate the challenges and obstacles in my life, may your powerful presence inspire me to persevere and overcome. Guide me towards the inner strength that I need to face any challenge with courage and resilience, and help me to be a source of strength and support for those around me.

Day 23: Hekate, goddess of the crossroads, I offer this prayer to you. May your guidance and wisdom be with me always, helping me to navigate the twists and turns of life with grace and resilience. Grant me the clarity and conviction to make the right choices and decisions, and may your presence infuse my being with the strength and courage to stay true to my path.

Day 24: Hekate, goddess of the night and the shadows, I call upon you to bless me with the courage and resilience that I need to face my fears and challenges. As I confront the dark and shadowy aspects of myself and the world around me, may your presence inspire me to tap into my own inner strength and rise up in triumph over my fears. Help me to embrace the shadows as a source of power and transformation, and guide me towards the light of my own inner wisdom and courage.

Day 25: Hekate, mistress of magic and mystery, I offer this prayer to you. May your potent energy infuse my intentions with magic and possibility, helping me to manifest my deepest desires and dreams. Guide me towards the path of success and fulfillment, and grant me the wisdom to tap into my own inner resources and creativity. May your blessings be upon me always, empowering me to create a life of magic and wonder.

Day 26: Hekate, guardian of the crossroads and keeper of the keys, I call upon your strength and courage as I face the challenges ahead. Guide me to the right path and help me to make the choices that will lead to success and prosperity.

Day 27: Hekate, wise and powerful goddess of magic, I offer this prayer to you. Help me to develop my spiritual gifts and talents, and guide me as I seek to understand the mysteries of the universe. Grant me the courage and strength to explore new realms of consciousness and unlock the secrets of the unseen world.

Day 28: Hekate, goddess of the moon and the night, I call upon your wisdom and guidance as I navigate the darkness of the unknown. Shine your light upon my path and guide me towards my destiny.

Day 29: Invocation: Hekate, queen of the underworld, I offer this prayer to you. Grant me the strength and power to confront my deepest fears and insecurities, and help me to overcome my doubts and embrace my true potential. Guide me through the darkness and into the light, so that I may emerge stronger and more confident.

Day 30: Hekate, goddess of the wild places, I call upon your primal energy and untamed power as I seek to connect with the natural world. Help me to find my place in the cycle of life and death, and to honor the earth and all its creatures.

Day 31: Hekate, goddess of the crossroads and the liminal spaces, I offer this prayer to you. As I embark on a new chapter of my life, guide me through the transitions and changes that lie ahead. Protect me as I journey through the unknown, and help me to stay focused on my goals and aspirations. Lead me towards a brighter future, filled with joy, love, and abundance.

Here's a new moon ritual for August:

Items needed:

- Black candle
- White candle
- Frankincense incense
- A piece of paper and pen
- A small cauldron or fire-safe dish
- A piece of string or ribbon

Steps:

1. Set up your altar with the black candle on the left side and the white candle on the right. Light the frankincense incense.

2. Sit quietly and take a few deep breaths to center yourself.

3. Light the black candle, and say: "Hekate, goddess of the crossroads, I call upon your strength and guidance. Please bless me with your power and help me overcome any challenges in my path."

4. Light the white candle, and say: "Hekate, goddess of the moon, I ask for your wisdom and intuition. Please guide me in making the right decisions and give me the strength to follow through."

5. Write down any fears, doubts, or insecurities you may have on the piece of paper. Take your time to really explore and identify what is holding you back.

6. Once you have finished writing, fold the piece of paper and tie it with the string or ribbon.

7. Hold the paper over the black candle and say: "Hekate, I offer these fears and doubts to you. Please help me release them and replace them with strength and courage."

8. Light the paper on fire using the black candle and let it burn in the cauldron or fire-safe dish. As it burns, repeat the affirmation: "I am strong and courageous. I have the power to overcome any obstacle in my path."

9. Sit with the white candle for a few more minutes, visualizing yourself embodying the strength and courage you seek. When you are ready, extinguish the candles and incense.

10. Take the ashes of the burned paper and scatter them outside, thanking Hekate for her guidance and strength.

May this ritual bring you the strength and courage you need to face any challenges ahead.

Chapter 10: Invocations and Prayers for September

As the season begins to shift towards autumn, we turn our attention towards finding balance, harmony, and peace in our lives. In this chapter, we will explore invocations and prayers to Hekate that can help us cultivate these qualities within ourselves and our surroundings.

September is a month of transition, and the energies of Hekate can help us navigate these changes with grace and ease. As we invoke her, we ask for her guidance in finding equilibrium and serenity, and for her blessings to bring balance to all areas of our lives.

Join us in this journey as we call upon the goddess of crossroads to help us find balance, harmony, and peace in our hearts, our relationships, and our communities.

Day 1: Hekate, goddess of the crossroads, I call upon you to bring balance and harmony to my life. May your presence help me find peace within myself, and guide me towards the path of equilibrium and stability.

Day 2: Hekate, mistress of transitions, I offer this prayer to you. May your guidance and protection help me find balance and stability as I move through the changes in my life. May your blessings bring harmony to my relationships and surroundings, and may I find peace within myself through your grace.

Day 3: Hekate, goddess of wisdom and intuition, I call upon you to help me find balance and harmony in my thoughts and emotions. May your light guide me towards peace, and may I feel your presence as I seek clarity and understanding.

Day 4: Hekate, mistress of the moon and the tides, I offer this prayer to you. May your guidance and protection help me find balance and harmony in the ebb and flow of my life. May your blessings bring peace to my heart and soul, and may I find strength and resilience through your grace.

Day 5: Hekate, goddess of the earth and the harvest, I call upon you to help me find balance and harmony in the abundance of my life. May your light guide me towards gratitude and contentment, and may I feel your presence as I reap the fruits of my labor.

Day 6: Hekate, mistress of the underworld and the unseen, I offer this prayer to you. May your guidance and protection help me find balance and harmony in the shadows of my life. May your blessings bring acceptance and healing to my heart, and may I find courage and strength through your grace.

Day 7: Hekate, goddess of magic and mystery, I call upon you to bless this day with your transformative power. May your magic help me find balance and harmony in all areas of my life, and may your mysteries guide me towards inner peace and serenity.

Day 8: Hekate, mistress of the crossroads, I offer this prayer to you. May your guidance and protection illuminate the path before me, and may your presence provide me with the courage and strength to face any challenges that come my way. Help me to find balance and harmony in the midst of uncertainty and to trust in the wisdom of your guidance.

Day 9: Hekate, goddess of the underworld, I call upon you to bless this day with your wisdom and insight. May your connection to the depths of the earth bring me a sense of grounding and stability, and may your knowledge of the mysteries of life and death help me find peace in the face of change.

Day 10: Hekate, mistress of the moon, I offer this prayer to you. May your gentle and nurturing energy bring me a sense of peace and tranquility, and may your gentle presence guide me towards balance and harmony. Help me to find rest and renewal in your light, and to trust in the cycles of the moon and the rhythms of nature.

Day 11: Hekate, goddess of crossroads and liminal spaces, I call upon you to help me find balance in my life. Guide me towards making decisions that bring harmony to my mind, body, and spirit, and help me to create peace within myself and in my relationships with others.

Day 12: Hekate, mistress of magic and sorcery, I offer this prayer to you. Please guide me towards finding balance in the use of my power, and help me to use it responsibly and with wisdom. May I create a harmonious relationship with the magic that flows through me, and use it for the greater good.

Day 13: Hekate, goddess of the underworld, I call upon you to help me find balance in my relationship with death and the afterlife. Guide me towards accepting the inevitability of death and embracing the cycles of life, death, and rebirth. Help me to create a harmonious relationship with the unseen realms, and to find peace in the knowledge that we are all connected through the cycle of life.

Day 14: Hekate, mistress of the moon, I offer this prayer to you. Please guide me towards finding balance in my connection to the lunar cycles. Help me to understand the phases of the moon and their influence on my emotions and energy levels. May I create a harmonious relationship with the moon, and use its energy for my growth and well-being.

Day 15: Hekate, goddess of the night, I call upon you to help me find balance in my relationship with darkness and the unknown. Guide me towards embracing the mysteries of the night and the secrets they hold, and help me to create a harmonious relationship with the shadows within myself. May I find peace in the knowledge that light and darkness are two sides of the same coin, and that both are necessary for balance and harmony.

Day 16: Hekate, mistress of magic and mystery, I offer this prayer to you. May your wisdom and power help me find balance in my life, and may your loving presence bring peace to my heart. Help me to stay centered and calm in the midst of life's challenges, and to trust in the beauty and perfection of the universe.

Day 17: Hekate, goddess of the crossroads, I call upon you to guide me towards a path of harmony and balance. Help me to make wise choices that support my physical, mental, emotional, and spiritual well-being, and guide me towards greater peace and serenity.

Day 18: Hekate, mistress of the night, I offer this prayer to you. May your healing energy bring balance to my dreams and subconscious, and may your loving presence bring peace to my soul. Help me to release any fears or anxieties that may be disrupting my rest, and to trust in the power of my dreams to guide me towards greater harmony and balance.

Day 19: Hekate, goddess of the moon, I call upon you to bring balance and harmony to my emotions. Help me to release any negative emotions or attachments that may be holding me back, and guide me towards greater peace and serenity.

Day 20: Hekate, mistress of the earth, I offer this prayer to you. May your healing energy bring balance and harmony to my physical body, and may your loving presence bring peace to my soul. Help me to release any tension or stress that may be causing me discomfort or pain, and to trust in the power of nature to guide me towards greater harmony and balance.

Day 21: Hekate, goddess of the underworld, I call upon you to help me find balance and harmony in my shadow self. Guide me towards greater self-awareness and self-acceptance, and help me to integrate all aspects of myself with love and compassion.

Day 22: Hekate, goddess of the crossroads, I call upon you to bless this day with your divine presence. May your wisdom guide me towards finding balance in my life, and may your light shine upon me as I seek harmony in all aspects of my being.

Day 23: Hekate, guardian of the crossroads, I offer this prayer to you. Please guide me towards balance and harmony in my life. May I find the strength to make decisions that are in alignment with my highest good and the greater good of all. Help me to find peace and fulfillment on my journey.

Day 24: Hekate, goddess of the moon and magic, I call upon you to help me find balance and harmony within myself. May your divine energy guide me towards a state of inner peace and calm, and help me to tap into my own intuitive wisdom.

Day 25: Hekate, mistress of the night and the mysteries, I offer this prayer to you. Please help me to find balance and harmony in my spiritual practice. May your divine energy guide me towards a deeper understanding of myself and the universe around me.

Day 26: Hekate, goddess of the sea and storms, I call upon you to help me find balance and harmony in my emotional life. May your divine energy calm the waters within me and help me to navigate any emotional storms that may arise.

Day 27: Hekate, mistress of the wilderness and the wild places, I offer this prayer to you. Please help me to find balance and harmony with nature. May your divine energy guide me towards a deeper connection with the natural world and a greater appreciation for the balance and harmony of all living things.

Day 28: Hekate, goddess of transitions and change, I call upon you to help me find balance and harmony in times of change. May your divine energy guide me through any transitions that I may face and help me to find stability and peace in the midst of change.

Day 29: Hekate, goddess of magic and mystery, I offer this prayer to you. May your wisdom and insight guide me towards balance and harmony in my life, and help me to cultivate a sense of peace and serenity within. Help me to see beyond the surface of things and to gain a deeper understanding of myself and the world around me. Thank you for your blessings.

Day 30: Hekate, goddess of the crossroads, I call upon you to bless me with your guidance and protection. As I stand at the crossroads of my life, help me to make decisions that are in alignment with my highest good and the greater good of all. Protect me on my journey and guide me towards a path of balance, harmony, and peace.

New Moon Ritual for September:

"Hekate, goddess of the moon and the night, I call upon you to bless this ritual with your divine presence. As we gather under the new moon, may your light guide us through the darkness and lead us towards the balance, strength, and courage we seek."

1. Set up your altar with symbols of balance, strength, and courage. You can include crystals such as amethyst, clear quartz, and tiger's eye, as well as candles and any other objects that hold personal significance for you.

2. Light the candles on your altar, and take a few deep breaths to ground yourself in the present moment.

3. Begin the ritual by reciting the following invocation to Hekate:

"Hekate, goddess of the moon and the night, We gather under your divine light. As we seek balance, strength, and courage anew, We call upon you to guide us through.

Lead us through the darkness of the night, And fill our hearts with your guiding light. May your wisdom and power help us find, The strength and balance we need to shine."

4. Take a moment to meditate on the areas of your life where you would like to find more balance, strength, and courage. Visualize yourself achieving your goals and feeling confident and empowered.

5. When you are ready, offer a prayer to Hekate, asking for her continued guidance and support on your journey towards balance and strength.

6. Close the ritual by thanking Hekate for her presence and blowing out the candles on your altar. Carry the energy of the ritual with you as you move forward, knowing that you have Hekate's guidance and protection on your path.

Chapter 11: Invocations and Prayers for October

As the seasons begin to shift and the veil between worlds grows thinner, October offers us an opportunity to explore the mysteries of the unknown. In this chapter, we turn to Hekate, goddess of magic and the liminal spaces, to guide us in our journey of self-discovery and spiritual growth. Through invocations and prayers, we seek her wisdom and guidance as we delve into the mystical realms of the unseen. May her light illuminate our path as we embrace the magic and mystery of this transformative time.

Day 1: Oh great Hekate, goddess of magic and the unknown, I call upon you to guide me on my path of mysticism. Help me to tap into the secrets of the universe and unlock the mysteries of the unknown.

Day 2: With your guidance, Hekate, I am able to see beyond the veil and access the magic that lies within. May your divine presence empower me and strengthen my connection to the mystical realm.

Day 3: As I embark on this journey of discovery, I ask for your guidance and protection, Hekate. Let your divine light guide me through the darkness and keep me safe as I explore the unknown.

Day 4: Oh powerful Hekate, goddess of the mystic arts, I pray that you bless me with the gifts of intuition, insight, and foresight. May I be able to discern the unseen and navigate the unknown with ease.

Day 5: I call upon your divine energy, Hekate, to infuse me with the power of magic. May I be able to work miracles and perform feats of wonder, all in your name.

Day 6: Hekate, goddess of the unknown, I pray that you help me to unlock the secrets of the universe and reveal the mysteries of the cosmos. May your divine wisdom illuminate my path.

Day 7: With your divine grace, Hekate, I am able to transcend the physical and explore the spiritual. May your presence guide me on this journey of mysticism and magic.

Day 8: Oh great Hekate, I pray that you help me to tap into the energies of the universe and harness their power for my own use. May I be able to work magic in your name and for the greater good.

Day 9: As I delve deeper into the unknown, I ask for your guidance, Hekate. May your divine light illuminate my path and lead me to greater understanding and wisdom.

Day 10: With your blessings, Hekate, I am able to see beyond the surface and access the deeper truths of the universe. May your divine presence guide me as I explore the mystical realm.

Day 11: I call upon your divine energy, Hekate, to help me master the arts of magic and mysticism. May your wisdom and knowledge empower me to become a true adept.

Day 12: Oh great Hekate, goddess of the unknown, I pray that you reveal to me the secrets of the universe and empower me to access its deepest mysteries.

Day 13: With your guidance and protection, Hekate, I am able to navigate the unknown with confidence and ease. May your divine light shine upon me always.

Day 14: I pray that you bless me with the ability to harness the power of magic and the unknown, Hekate. May your divine energy empower me to work wonders and achieve great things in your name.

Day 15: Oh Hekate, goddess of the crossroads, I call upon you to guide me through the unknown paths that lie ahead. May your divine presence protect me and illuminate my way.

Day 16: With your blessings, Hekate, I am able to tap into the deep well of my own inner magic. May your wisdom and guidance help me to access and channel this power for good.

Day 17: I pray that you help me to embrace the mystery and uncertainty of life, Hekate. May your divine light show me the way forward and inspire me to seek the truth that lies beyond.

Day 18: Oh great Hekate, goddess of the moon and magic, I ask that you fill me with your divine energy and awaken my mystical senses. May I be able to connect with the unseen world and receive its wisdom.

Day 19: I call upon your power, Hekate, to help me manifest my deepest desires and intentions. May your divine energy infuse my magic and help me to create positive change in my life.

Day 20: With your guidance, Hekate, I am able to unlock the secrets of the universe and access its hidden knowledge. May your divine wisdom illuminate my path and reveal the mysteries of the cosmos.

Day 21: Oh great Hekate, goddess of magic and mystery, I pray that you help me to release any fear or doubt that may hold me back. May your divine presence fill me with courage and confidence as I walk the path of the unknown.

Day 22: I call upon your power, Hekate, to help me balance the light and the dark within me. May your divine energy guide me towards a harmonious relationship with the unknown forces of the universe.

Day 23: With your blessings, Hekate, I am able to access my own inner wisdom and intuition. May your divine light help me to trust myself and navigate the unknown with grace and ease.

Day 24: I pray that you help me to connect with the spirits and energies that surround me, Hekate. May your divine presence facilitate my communication with the unseen world and deepen my understanding of its mysteries.

Day 25: Oh great Hekate, goddess of the crossroads and magic, I ask that you help me find my own unique path through the unknown. May your divine guidance lead me towards my true purpose and destiny.

Day 26: I call upon your power, Hekate, to help me release any limiting beliefs or negative patterns that may block my progress. May your divine energy empower me to overcome any obstacle and move forward with confidence.

Day 27: With your blessings, Hekate, I am able to connect with the wisdom of the ages and access the ancient knowledge that lies within me. May your divine light illuminate my path and show me the way forward.

Day 28: I pray that you help me to tap into the power of the collective consciousness, Hekate. May your divine presence guide me towards a deeper understanding of the interconnectedness of all things.

Day 29: Oh great Hekate, goddess of the moon and magic, I ask that you bless me with the gifts of intuition and foresight. May your divine energy empower me to see beyond the veil and access the wisdom of the unseen world.

Day 30: I call upon your power, Hekate, to help me embrace the unknown and trust in the universe's plan for me. May your divine guidance fill me with faith and optimism as I journey towards my highest good.

Day 31: With your blessings, Hekate, I am able to celebrate the magic and mystery of life. May your divine light shine upon me and inspire me to live each day with purpose and passion, knowing that you are always with me and guiding me towards my highest good. Thank you, Hekate, for your constant love and support. May I continue to honor you and your wisdom in all that I do. Hail Hekate!

Here is a new moon ritual for October:

You will need:

- A black candle
- A piece of paper and pen
- A bowl of water
- Incense (optional)

Preparation: Choose a quiet and sacred space for your ritual. Cleanse the area with incense or sage, and create a small altar with the black candle, paper and pen, and bowl of water. You may also wish to add any other items that feel meaningful to you, such as crystals or statues of Hekate.

The Ritual:

1. Begin by taking a few deep breaths to center yourself. Light the black candle and focus your gaze on the flame.

2. Call upon Hekate, goddess of magic and mystery, to join you in your ritual. You may use the following invocation or create one of your own:

"Hekate, great goddess of the crossroads and the unknown, I invite you to be present with me now. Bless me with your wisdom and guidance as I journey into the mysteries of the new moon."

3. Write down on the piece of paper any fears, doubts, or negative patterns that you wish to release. Be honest and specific in your writing.

4. Once you have finished writing, fold the paper and hold it over the bowl of water. Call upon Hekate to assist you in releasing these negative energies. Visualize the energy of your fears and doubts flowing from your body and into the paper.

5. Drop the paper into the water and watch as it dissolves. Imagine Hekate cleansing and purifying your energy with the water, washing away all negativity and clearing the path for new beginnings.

6. Take a moment to reflect on what you wish to manifest during this new moon cycle. Write down your intentions for the upcoming month, focusing on what you wish to create and attract into your life.

7. Hold the paper with your intentions over the flame of the candle, allowing the fire to ignite your desires and infuse them with Hekate's divine energy.

8. Thank Hekate for her presence and guidance in your ritual. Blow out the candle and close the space.

Chapter 12: Prayers for November

As the year comes to a close and we approach the holiday season, it is important to take time to reflect on all that we have to be thankful for. In this chapter, we will explore various invocations and prayers that can help us cultivate a sense of gratitude and appreciation for the abundance in our lives. These practices can help us to deepen our connection with the divine and foster a spirit of thankfulness that can carry us through the holiday season and into the new year. Join me as we explore the power of gratitude in our spiritual practice.

Day 1: Glorious Hekate, I give thanks for the abundance that surrounds me. Your blessings have bestowed upon me everything that I need.

Day 2: Mighty Hekate, I am grateful for the marvels of nature that inspire me every day. Your creation is a manifestation of your divine essence.

Day 3: Revered Hekate, I appreciate the relationships in my life that support and enrich me. Thank you for the love and companionship of my family and friends.

Day 4: Respected Hekate, I give thanks for the trials and lessons I have experienced, for they have made me stronger and wiser.

Day 5: Omnipotent Hekate, I am grateful for the liberty to express myself, to be who I am without restraint. Your teachings have instilled in me the courage to be true to myself.

Day 6: Enchanting Hekate, I appreciate the power of my intuition, the ability to sense and perceive beyond what is visible. Your guidance has honed my inner voice.

Day 7: Majestic Hekate, I give thanks for the opportunities that have come my way, for they have opened doors that I never thought possible.

Day 8: Divine Hekate, I am grateful for the splendor of nature that nurtures and sustains me. Your abundant gifts fill me with wonder and gratitude.

Day 9: Inspirational Hekate, I appreciate the strength of my spirit, the ability to endure and overcome challenges. Your tutelage has given me the resilience to face adversities.

Day 10: Mysterious Hekate, I give thanks for the beauty of the night sky that captivates and fascinates me. Your secrets fill me with awe and reverence.

Day 11: Celebrated Hekate, I am grateful for the joys that fill my life, for they remind me of the goodness in the world. Your blessings have filled my heart with happiness and contentment.

Day 12: Creative Hekate, I appreciate the artistic inspiration that flows through me, the capacity to express myself through various mediums. Your influence fuels my creativity.

Day 13: Beneficent Hekate, I give thanks for the nourishment that sustains my body, the sustenance that keeps me healthy and vital. Your generosity is boundless.

Day 14: Harmonious Hekate, I am grateful for the power of music that elevates and uplifts me, that brings me solace and joy. Your rhythms and melodies move me deeply.

Day 15: Strengthening Hekate, I appreciate the potency of my voice, the capacity to communicate and express myself assertively. Your guidance has given me the confidence to speak my truth.

Day 16: Wise Hekate, I give thanks for the lessons of my ancestors, the knowledge that has been passed down through generations. Your wisdom endures and guides me.

Day 17: Transformative Hekate, I am grateful for the magic of change, the ability to evolve and grow beyond my limitations. Your energy facilitates my transformation.

Day 18: Inspiring Hekate, I appreciate the role models in my life, the people who inspire and motivate me to be my best self. Your guidance helps me to recognize the greatness in others.

Day 19: Protective Hekate, I give thanks for the safety and security that surrounds me, the protection that keeps me from harm. Your guardianship watches over me always.

Day 20: Healing Hekate, I am grateful for the restoration of my body, mind, and spirit, the power of healing that transforms me. Your grace brings me comfort and relief.

Day 21: Gracious Hekate, I appreciate the acts of kindness and compassion that I have received, the generosity of others that lifts me up. Your influence fosters goodwill and benevolence.

Day 22: Joyful Hekate, I give thanks for the laughter and playfulness in my life, the moments of delight that bring me joy. Your spirit of merriment infuses my days with happiness.

Day 23: Patient Hekate, I am grateful for the virtues of patience and perseverance that enable me to endure challenges and obstacles. Your teachings give me the strength to persist.

Day 24: Compassionate Hekate, I appreciate the empathy and understanding that I receive from others, the ability to connect and relate to those around me. Your influence promotes empathy and compassion.

Day 25: Generous Hekate, I give thanks for the blessings of abundance that I have received, the opportunities to share my prosperity with others. Your generosity inspires me to give back.

Day 26: Faithful Hekate, I am grateful for the guidance and support that I have received in times of need, the divine intervention that has saved me. Your faithfulness brings me hope and trust.

Day 27: Confident Hekate, I appreciate the courage and self-assurance that I possess, the ability to face challenges with conviction. Your teachings give me the confidence to believe in myself.

Day 28: Transcendent Hekate, I give thanks for the spiritual experiences that have transformed me, the moments of divine connection that elevate me. Your transcendence lifts me to higher realms.

Day 29: Enlightening Hekate, I am grateful for the knowledge and insight that I have gained, the wisdom that has expanded my understanding. Your teachings illuminate my path.

Day 30: Grateful Hekate, I appreciate the opportunity to express my gratitude and thanksgiving for all that I have received. Your presence in my life fills me with abundance and blessings.

New Moon ritual for November

Set up an altar with candles, incense, crystals, and any other tools you feel connected to. Sit comfortably in front of your altar and take several deep breaths to center yourself.

Invocation: Oh Hekate, Queen of the Night, we call upon you on this sacred night of the new moon. You who stand at the crossroads of life and death, magic and mystery, we ask for your presence and blessings.

Light the candles and incense, and place your crystals on the altar. Close your eyes and envision a glowing white light surrounding you, protecting and grounding you.

Prayer: Great Hekate, we come before you with humble hearts and open minds. We give thanks for all the blessings that have come our way, and we ask for your guidance as we embark on a new journey.

We ask for your strength and courage to face the unknown, for your wisdom and intuition to make the right decisions, and for your protection and guidance as we navigate through the darkness.

As we stand at the crossroads of life, we ask for your divine intervention to help us choose the path that is in alignment with our true purpose and destiny.

Closing: We offer you our gratitude and thanks, Hekate, for your presence and blessings. As we extinguish the candles and incense, we ask that your energy continue to guide and protect us on our journey. So mote it be.

Chapter 13: Prayers for December

As the year draws to a close, it is a time of reflection, introspection, and spiritual growth. In this chapter, we turn to Hekate, the goddess of the crossroads, magic, and wisdom, to guide us on this journey of self-discovery and transformation.

Through invoking Hekate, we ask for her divine guidance and wisdom to help us reflect on the past year and make sense of our experiences. We seek her support as we engage in introspection, looking inward to understand our thoughts, feelings, and desires.

As we connect with Hekate in this way, we open ourselves to spiritual growth and transformation, allowing ourselves to release what no longer serves us and embrace the opportunities for growth and expansion that lie ahead.

May these prayers to Hekate inspire you to deepen your connection with her, and to embark on a journey of reflection, introspection, and spiritual growth in the month of December.

Day 1: Oh Hekate, guide me on my journey of reflection, as I look back on the past year with clarity and insight. Help me to see the lessons and opportunities for growth that lie within my experiences.

Day 2: Great Hekate, as I engage in introspection, help me to connect with my inner wisdom and intuition. May I find the answers and guidance that I seek within myself.

Day 3: Hekate, goddess of magic and transformation, help me to release what no longer serves me, making space for new beginnings and growth.

Day 4: Oh Hekate, grant me the strength and courage to face my fears and shadows, and to embrace the opportunities for growth and transformation that lie ahead.

Day 5: Great Hekate, as I reflect on my relationships, help me to see the lessons and growth opportunities within them. May I approach all my relationships with honesty, compassion, and grace.

Day 6: Hekate, goddess of the crossroads, guide me as I navigate through the choices and decisions that lie ahead. May I make choices that are in alignment with my highest good and true purpose.

Day 7: Oh Hekate, as I reflect on my spiritual path, help me to deepen my connection with the divine and to awaken to my true nature.

Day 8: Great Hekate, help me to cultivate inner peace and stillness as I engage in meditation and spiritual practice. May I connect with my higher self and access the wisdom and guidance within.

Day 9: Hekate, goddess of wisdom, guide me as I seek to expand my knowledge and understanding of the mysteries of the universe. May I approach all learning with an open mind and heart.

Day 10: Oh Hekate, help me to embrace the transformative power of ritual and ceremony, using these tools to deepen my connection with the divine and to create positive change in my life.

Day 11: Great Hekate, as I reflect on my career and life purpose, help me to align my actions with my values and to pursue my passions with dedication and perseverance.

Day 12: Hekate, goddess of magic, help me to tap into my own inner power and to manifest my desires in alignment with my highest good.

Day 13: Oh Hekate, as I engage in self-care and self-love, help me to recognize and honor my own worth and to cultivate a sense of inner peace and contentment.

Day 14: Great Hekate, guide me as I seek to heal and release any emotional wounds or traumas, allowing myself to experience greater joy, peace, and happiness.

Day 15: Hekate, goddess of the crossroads, help me to recognize the opportunities for growth and expansion that lie within every challenge or obstacle.

Day 16: Oh Hekate, as I reflect on my connection to the natural world, help me to deepen my appreciation for the beauty and wonder of the earth, and to become a steward of the environment.

Day 17: Great Hekate, as I seek to connect with my ancestors and honor their legacy, help me to cultivate a sense of gratitude and reverence for their guidance and wisdom.

Day 18: Hekate, goddess of magic and transformation, help me to let go of limiting beliefs and patterns, and to embrace the opportunities for growth and expansion that lie ahead.

Day 19: Oh Hekate, as I engage in creative expression, help me to tap into my own unique gifts and talents, and to share them with the world in a way that brings joy and peace.

Day 20: Hekate, as I look back on this year, I am grateful for the challenges and the growth that they brought. May I continue to learn from my experiences and move forward with greater wisdom and understanding. Guide me on my path of spiritual growth and help me to embrace the changes that lie ahead.

Day 21: Oh great Hekate, as I reflect on my past, may I not dwell on my mistakes or regrets, but instead focus on the lessons that they have taught me. May I have the courage to forgive myself and others, and move forward with an open heart.

Day 22: Hekate, as I look within, may I see the light that shines within me. Help me to cultivate self-love and self-acceptance, so that I may radiate this love outwards to others. May I recognize my own worth and value, and honor the divinity within myself.

Day 23: Oh wise Hekate, as I contemplate my spiritual journey, may I have the patience and perseverance to continue even when the path is difficult. Help me to trust in the journey and have faith that I am exactly where I need to be. Guide me towards greater understanding and enlightenment.

Day 24: Hekate, as I prepare to celebrate the winter solstice, may I honor the darkness that comes before the light. Help me to embrace the stillness and the quiet, and use this time for reflection and introspection. May I find inner peace and clarity during this sacred time.

Day 25: On this day of celebration, I offer my gratitude to you, Hekate, for your presence in my life. Thank you for guiding me on my path and for helping me to grow and evolve. May your light shine bright within me, and may I carry this light out into the world.

Day 26: Hekate, as I look towards the new year, may I set intentions that align with my highest self and my true purpose. Help me to let go of any fears or doubts that may hold me back, and instead focus on my strength and my potential. May I step into the new year with confidence and clarity.

Day 27: Oh great Hekate, as I contemplate the mysteries of the universe, may I see the interconnectedness of all things. Help me to recognize the divine spark within all beings, and to honor the diversity and beauty of the world around me. May I cultivate compassion and empathy in my heart.

Day 28: Hekate, as I meditate on my own mortality, may I live my life with purpose and intention. Help me to make the most of each moment, and to cherish the relationships and experiences that I have in this lifetime. May I leave a positive impact on the world around me.

Day 29: Oh wise Hekate, as I seek spiritual growth and evolution, may I remember that the journey is never-ending. Help me to embrace the process, and to find joy and fulfillment in the pursuit of greater understanding. May I always remain curious and open-minded.

Day 30: Hekate, as I conclude this month of reflection and introspection, may I carry the lessons that I have learned with me into the new year. Help me to continue to grow and evolve, and to cultivate a deeper connection with the divine. May I always be guided by your wisdom and your light.

Hekate New Moon Ritual for December

Preparation:

- Set up a small altar with a black and white candle, an incense burner, and a glass of wine.

- Light the incense burner and prepare to light the candles.

Opening:

- Stand before the altar and take a deep breath.

- Call upon Hekate, goddess of the crossroads, magic, and wisdom, to join you in this ritual.

- Light the black candle, saying: "Hekate, goddess of the unknown and mystery, we invoke you with this candle."

- Light the white candle, saying: "Hekate, goddess of clarity and guidance, we invoke you with this candle."

Offerings:

- Hold up the incense burner and say: "Hekate, we offer you this incense as a symbol of our prayers and offerings."

- Hold up the glass of wine and say: "Hekate, we offer you this wine as a symbol of the richness of our experiences and the blood of life."

Invocation:

- Stand before the altar with your hands raised.

- Call upon Hekate, saying: "Hekate, goddess of the crossroads, magic, and wisdom, we invoke you in this new moon ritual of gratitude and invocation. We thank you for guiding us through the unknown and for the spiritual growth and experiences we have had in the past year."

Reflection and Intention:

- Take a moment to reflect on the past year and the spiritual growth you have experienced.

- Set intentions for the coming year, asking Hekate for guidance and blessings.

- Speak your intentions out loud, knowing that Hekate is listening and guiding you.

Closing:

- Thank Hekate for joining you in this ritual.

- Blow out the candles, saying: "Hekate, we thank you for your presence and guidance in our lives. May your wisdom and insight continue to bless us in the coming year."

Chapter 14: Conclusion

As we come to the end of this book, we reflect on the journey we have taken with Hekate over the course of the year. We have explored different aspects of her mythology and symbolism, and delved into various practices and rituals to connect with her energy.

Through this journey, we have gained insights into ourselves and the mysteries of life. We have been guided by Hekate through the crossroads of our personal paths, and have grown in our understanding of magic, mysticism, and the unknown.

As we close this chapter, we encourage you to continue connecting with Hekate beyond the pages of this book. Remember that she is always present, waiting for us to reach out to her for guidance and support. Continue to work with her in your daily life, incorporating the practices and rituals that resonate with you.

Before we end, let us offer a final prayer and invocation to Hekate for blessings and guidance in the journey ahead.

Hekate, goddess of the crossroads, magic, and wisdom, We offer you our gratitude and thanks for your presence and guidance throughout this journey. May your wisdom and insight continue to bless us as we navigate the unknown paths of life. Guide us through the crossroads of our personal paths, Illuminate the mysteries of life, And lead us towards our true purpose and destiny. We ask for your blessings and protection as we continue our journey with you.

Hail Hekate!

A Hymn to Hekate

Oh Hekate, goddess of many names,
Your power and wisdom we forever acclaim.

Mistress of the Crossroads, where paths do meet,
Guide us through the unknown with your light so sweet.

Queen of the Witches, with magic so bright,
Your spells and incantations grant us sight.

Torchbearer, illuminating the night,
With your radiance, our fears take flight.

Chthonia, goddess of the earth below,
You show us the mysteries that lie low.

Enodia, goddess of the roads and ways,
Your guidance leads us through life's many phase.

Kourotrophos, nurturing mother divine,
You nourish our souls and hearts with your wine.

Soteira, savior in times of need,
Your protection and care, we gratefully heed.

Propolos, leading us towards our fate,
You help us choose our path, never too late.

Trioditis, three-faced goddess so wise,
Your triple form, a reflection of the skies.

Phosphoros, bringing dawn's golden light,
Your radiance banishes darkness from sight.

Chthonia, Enodia, Kourotrophos, Soteira, Propolos,
Trioditis, Phosphoros, oh Hekate, hear our call,
We sing your praises, we honor your name,
Your power and wisdom, forever we proclaim!

Full Moon Invocation Ritual to Hekate:

Preparation:

- Set up an altar with an image or statue of Hekate, candles, incense, and offerings such as wine, honey, or flowers.

- Take a few deep breaths to ground and center yourself.

Invocation:

- Light the candles and incense.

- Face the altar and call upon Hekate with the following invocation:

Hekate, powerful and wise goddess, Queen of the night and guide of the lost, You who hold the keys to the mysteries, We call upon you on this full moon night.

Come to us, Hekate, With your torches blazing bright, Lead us through the darkness And into the wisdom of the light.

Offerings:

- Offer the wine, honey, or flowers to Hekate as a symbol of your gratitude and devotion.

- Take a moment to reflect on your intentions and desires for the full moon.

Closing:

- Close the ritual with the following words:

Hekate, we thank you for your presence And for the guidance you have bestowed. As the moon shines its fullest light, May your blessings continue to flow. Hail Hekate!

Made in the USA
Monee, IL
03 August 2023

40410081R00129